Preface

Speaking Spanish with ease and effectiveness cannot be achieved merely by learning vocabulary and grammar rules. Spanish, like all living languages, has developed a rich variety of grammatical nuances and idiomatic expressions that, when put to use, give liveliness and natural color to both speech *and* writing.

Guide to Spanish Idioms provides, in an easy-to-use format, all the expressions and shades of meaning needed to speak and write Spanish naturally. First, there is a list of 2,500 Spanish idioms followed by an index for cross-reference in English. In addition, a variety of special sections on language difficulties, ambiguities, and common errors highlight "trouble spots" of the Spanish language for English speakers.

This guide is not intended to replace basic textbooks, grammars, or dictionaries. Instead, it supplements these sources with information on idiomatic expressions and grammatical ambiguities otherwise found in scattered references or not at all.

Students of Spanish, for example, learn early in their studies that *la mano* is the only feminine Spanish noun that ends in -*o*, a generally masculine ending. Later, however, they discover that there are other feminine nouns with masculine endings, as well as masculine nouns with feminine endings. They will also come across nouns that take on different meanings depending on whether they assume the masculine or feminine gender. But where can one find these nouns listed? This book provides such information and presents it in a conveniently arranged, easy-to-use format.

Other common difficulties of the Spanish language dealt with in the book include the problem of "false friends" (Spanish words similar to words in English but having different meanings), special meanings of reflexive verbs, the intricate terms for family relationships, and many others summarized for the user in the Table of Contents on the following page.

Nonetheless, as the title of the book implies, the principal objective of *Guide to Spanish Idioms* is to present a carefully compiled collection of more than 2,500 idiomatic phrases and sayings that are part of the everyday speech of native Spanish speakers. Without colorful expressions such as *llover a cántaros* (to rain cats and dogs), *dar un portazo* (to slam the door), or *tener*

iii

malas pulgas (to be bad tempered), Spanish, even if grammatically correct, would seem mechanical and lifeless to native speakers. The idioms presented in this collection will thus add character and expressiveness to language structures learned from a textbook.

Guide to Spanish Idioms will serve as a valuable resource to a wide variety of users: first of all, quite naturally, to students and teachers of Spanish, but also to all libraries, businesses, government agencies, as well as to tourists visiting Spanish-speaking countries. It is also useful to Spanish speakers learning English as a second or foreign language.

With its wealth of clearly presented materials, *Guide to Spanish Idioms* is an indispensable and comprehensive reference for all those seeking to communicate more effectively and naturally in Spanish.

CONTENTS

(continued on next page)

A SELECTED LIST OF
SPANISH IDIOMS AND PHRASES
(SPANISH-TO-ENGLISH)

Introduction

Since there are many thousands of idioms in the Spanish language, this list (of 2,500) must be highly subjective (i.e., a matter of personal choices). Therefore it is inevitable that each reader will see examples he would have omitted and think of omissions of idioms he could have included, had he prepared such a list.

With only a few exceptions, this listing includes only idioms or phrases of a few words in length and excludes a vast number of proverbs and other lengthy idiomatic expressions.

SECTION I omits also many (but not all) of the Spanish idioms which can be translated word-for-word to an English expression. Examples of such exclusions are: **ahora o nunca, constar de, día por día, en vano,** etc. **"Tarde o temprano"** is a borderline case, included in SECTION I only because the word order in English is the reverse of that in Spanish. A few rather obvious phrases are included for somewhat subtle reasons, — such as their general usefulness or in order to complete a series (e.g., **tren correo, tren mixto,** etc.).

It will be readily apparent that many entries in this section consist of only two words, one of which may be: **a, con, de, en, para, por, que,** etc., used as either the first word or the second. These entries are significant in that they show the correct choice to go with the other word of the couplet. To emphasize this important aspect of SECTION I, note the following examples of "unexpected" translations when one has in mind only the more "usual" translation of the auxiliary word:

(1)	**a casa** has a meaning different from **en casa.**
(2)	**dar a** = "to look towards or out upon."
(3)	**dar a luz** = "to give birth to or to publish."
(4)	**tener a raya** = "to keep in bounds."
(5)	**casarse con** = "to marry (someone)." The idiom is not translated "marry with."
(6)	**ni con mucho** = "not by far."
(7)	**despedirse de** = "to say goodbye to."
(8)	**tener ganas de** = "to feel like."
(9)	**más de** = "more than."
(10)	**reírse de** = "to laugh at."
(11)	**vestido de** = "dressed in."
(12)	**vivir de sus uñas** = "to live by stealing."
(13)	**tener que** = "to have to."
(14)	**decir para su coleto** = "to say to oneself."
(15)	**por ciento** = "per cent."

(16) **por** dentro = "<u>on</u> the inside."

(17) **por** la mañana = "<u>in</u> the morning."

(18) **al por** menor = "<u>at</u> retail or <u>in</u> small quantities, etc."

The correct choice between **"para"** and **"por"** requires considerable study. Because of space limitations, the examples in SECTION I can cover only a small portion of the distinctions between these two words.

The entries in SECTION I are numbered serially under each letter of the alphabet. The alphabetized English equivalents in SECTION II show these numbers as A 1, A 2, - - -,B 1, B 2, etc., i.e., serialized under each letter of the alphabet. It is important to note that the alphabetizing in SECTION I follows a word-by-word plan (i.e., 1st word, 2nd word, etc.); whereas SECTION II follows a strictly letter-by-letter order. (There are good justifications for this alphabetizing difference which should become apparent to the student.) For example, in SECTION I the expression **"agua de mar"** (A 171) precedes **"agua delgada"** (A 172), whereas the reverse sequence would ensue if the letter-by-letter order of SECTION II were applied.

The word "re" is used occasionally in the sense of "with regard to."

The meanings of certain abbreviations are as follows:

<u>fam.</u> = familiar form

<u>imp.</u> = imperative (verb form)

<u>inf.</u> = infinitive (verb form)

<u>subj.</u> = subjunctive (verb form)

The English word "or" is used in SECTION I for presenting alternative Spanish idioms (in preference to the Spanish "o") and is in light face to show that it is an English word. The abbreviations given above are in light face and also underlined to show that they are abbreviations of English words.

The use of the asterisk (*) in SECTION I —

In learning the Spanish idioms it is frequently helpful to know both the literal and free translations to English. Instead of cluttering SECTION I with literal translations (many of which would be obvious to the student who has a moderately good Spanish vocabulary), a list of some of the most interesting literal translations is provided as APPENDIX A. Each entry of SECTION I that has a counterpart in APPENDIX A is marked with an asterisk (*) preceding the entry number.

If the student is stimulated by the examples marked with an asterisk(*) to look up the literal translations of other Spanish idioms that are not readily apparent to him, he will find the effort worthwhile.

The use of parentheses ( ) —

Parentheses are used in several ways (especially in SECTIONS I and II). However there should be little chance of confusion because of the inherent structure or content. As a preliminary guide, the following notes may prove helpful.

Parentheses are used to show:

1. An alternative masculine or feminine noun, pronoun or adjective form. Example: SECTION I, M 40, **me alegro mucho de verlo(a).**

2. An alternative word or idiom which can be used without materially affecting the translation. Example: SECTION I, C 71 **"certificado (or fe, or partida) de nacimiento"** means that **"certificado de nacimiento," "fe de nacimiento"** or **"partida de nacimiento,"** are all translated as synonyms for "birth certificate."

3. A word (e.g., preposition) frequently, but not always, used in an idiomatic expression. Example: SECTION I, A 65, **"a lo largo (de)"** where **"a lo largo"** simply means "alongside," and **"a lo largo de"** means "alongside of."

4. Optional expansions. Example: SECTION I, P 38, **"para siempre (+ jamás),"** where **"para siempre"** = "forever" and **"para siempre jamás"** = "forever and ever."

5. That the idiom is completed by the addition of a verb form such as an infinitive. Example: SECTION I, A 189 **"al (+ inf.)"** = "on doing something."

6. A conventional (and obvious) parenthetical explanation. Example: SECTION I, A 119 **"a que"** meaning "I bet" (not a real wager).

7. That certain English words (cf. SECTION II) to wit "a," "the," "of," and "to" are frequently (but not always) enclosed in parentheses and disregarded in the alphabetizing procedure. The "(to)" in SECTION II preceding verbs is desirable in that it readily indicates a following verb rather than a noun or other speech form.

A

1 **A bordo**
On board

2 **A buena hora**
On time

*3 **A buen santo te encomiendas**
To bark up the wrong tree

4 **A cada[1] momento**
Continually, frequently

5 **A cada[1] paso**
At every turn (or step)

6 **A cada[1] rato**
Each time, all the time

7 **A cambio de**
In exchange for

8 **A campo raso**
In the open

9 **A campo traviesa**
Cross country

10 **A casa**
Home

11 **A causa de**
On account of

12 **A ciegas**
Blindly

* See Appendix A

[1] "cada" is an invariable adjective

13 **A** (or **De**) **ciencia cierta**
With certainty

14 **¿A cómo se vende?**
At what price? How much is?

15 **A consecuencia de**
As a result of

16 **A continuación**
Below, as follows

*17 **A contrapelo**
Against the grain

18 **A crédito**
On credit

19 **¿A cuánto(s) estamos?**
What is the date?

20 **A deshora(s)**
At all hours, unexpectedly

21 **A despecho de**
In spite of

22 **A duras penas**
With great difficulty

23 **A escape**
Rapidly, at full speed,
at full sail

24 **A escondidas**
On the sly, under cover

25 **A escondidas de**
Without the knowledge of

26 **A eso de**
At about

27 **A espaldas**
Behind one's back

28 **A falta de**
For want of

29 **A fin de cuentas**
After all, in the final analysis

30 **A fin de que**
In order that, so that

31 **A fines de**
Late, towards the end of a
period (week, etc.).

32 **A flor de**
Flush with

33 **A flote**
Afloat

34 **A fondo**
Fully, thoroughly

35 **A fuerza de**
By force of, by dint of

36 **A gatas**
On all fours, crawling

37 **A guisa de**
Like, in the manner of

38 **A hurto**
On the sly, stealthily

39 **A instancias de**
At the request of

40 **A la antigüita**
Old-fashioned

41 **A la buena (mala)**
Willingly (unwillingly)

42 **A la buena de Dios**
Without malice, without plan,
at random

43 **A la caída del sol** (or **de la
tarde**)
At sunset

44 **A la carrera**
In haste, on the run

45 **A la derecha**
To the right

46 **A la fuerza**
By force

47 **A la izquierda**
To the left

48 **A la larga**
In the long run, slowly

49 **A la moda**
Up-to-date, in the latest
fashion

50 **A la noche**
Tonight, at night

*51 **A la postre**
At last

52 **A la redonda (or En redondo)**
All around, round about

53 **A la sazón**
Then, at that time

54 **A la ventura**
Aimlessly, haphazardly, at random

55 **A la verdad**
In truth, in earnest

56 **A la vez**
Together, at the same time

57 **A la vista de**
In plain view of

58 **A la voluntad**
At will, as you like

59 **A la vuelta de**
Around the corner, on returning

60 **A la vuelta de la esquina**
Around the corner

61 **A la vuelta de los años**
Within a few years

62 **A lado de**
Beside

63 **A las claras**
Clearly, openly, frankly, publicly

64 **A las mil maravillas**
Beautifully, in no trouble

65 **A lo largo (de)**
Along, alongside of, lengthwise, at full length

66 **A lo lejos**
In the distance

67 **A lo más**
At most, at worst

68 **A lo mejor**
Perhaps, maybe

69 **A lo sumo**
At the most

*70 **A los cuatro vientos**
In all directions

71 **A los pocos meses**
After a few months

72 **A (la) manera de**
Like, in the style of

73 **A mano**
By hand, at hand, hand-made

74 **A mar de**
A lot of, lots of

75 **Además de**
In addition to

76 **A más no poder**
To the utmost, full blast

77 **A más tardar**
At the very latest

78 **A más ver (or Hasta más ver).**
Goodbye.

79 **A mediados de**
About the middle of the (day, week, etc.), during the (week, etc.)

80 **A medida que**
As, in proportion as

81 **A medio camino**
Halfway (to a place)

82 **A medio hacer**
Incomplete, half-done

83 **A menos que**
Unless

84 **A menudo**
Often

85 **A merced de**
At the mercy (or expense) of

86 **A mi entender**
In my opinion, as I understand it

87 A mi modo de ver
In my opinion

88 A mi no me la pega
You can't fool me

89 ¡A mí que!
 What's that to me? So what?

90 A montones
In abundance, heaps

91 A ninguna parte
Nowhere

92 A no ser que
Unless

93 A ojo
By sight, by guess

94 A ojos cerrados
Blindly

95 A ojos vistas
Visibly, clearly

96 A oscuras (or A obscuras)
In the dark

97 A partir de
As of, beginning on

98 A partir de hoy
From today on

99 A pedir de boca
Exactly as desired

100 A perder
To spoil

101 A pesar de (todo)
In spite of (everything)

102 A pesar de que
In spite of the fact that

103 A pie
On foot, by foot

*104 A piedra y lodo
Shut tight

105 A plazo
On credit, by installments

106 A plomo
Vertical

107 A poco
Shortly after

108 A pocos pasos
At a short distance

109 A porfía
With great insistence

110 A primera luz
At dawn

111 A principios de
Towards, early in, about the
first of (day, week, etc.)

112 A propósito
By the way, apropos, suitable

113 A prueba de
— proof, safe against

114 A prueba de incendio
Fireproof

115 A puerta cerrada
Secretly, behind closed doors

116 A punto fijo
With certainty

117 A pura fuerza
By sheer force

118 A puros gritos
By just shouting

119 A que
I bet - - - (not a real wager)

120 ¡A que no!
I bet you don't!

121 ¿A qué viene eso?
What is the point of that?

***122 A quema ropa (or A
quemarropa)**
Very close, point blank,
without warning

123 A raíz de
Soon after, close to

124 A ras de (or Al ras con)
Flush (or even) with

125 A ratos
From time to time, at times

126 **A ratos perdidos**
In (at) odd or spare moments

127 **A razón de**
At the rate of

128 **A rienda suelta**
Free reign, violently, swiftly

129 **A saber**
Namely, that is

130 **A sabiendas**
Knowingly, consciously

131 **A salvo**
Safe, unharmed

132 **A sangre fría**
In cold blood

133 **A secas**
Plain, alone, simply, to the
point

134 **A semejanza de**
In the manner of

135 **A su (debido) tiempo**
In due course or time

136 **A sus órdenes**
At your service, "Present",
"Here"

137 **A tiempo**
On time, in time

138 **A toda costa**
By all means, at whatever
cost

139 **A toda hora**
At any time, at all times

140 **A toda prisa**
At greatest speed

141 **A toda vela**
Under full sail, at full speed

142 **A todas luces**
By all means, anyway you
look at it

143 **A todo correr**
At full speed

144 **A todo trance**
At all costs

145 **A todo trapo**
At full sail, speedily

146 **A traición**
Deceitfully, treacherously

147 **A través de**
Across, through

148 **A última hora**
At the last moment

149 **A (or En or De) ultramar**
Overseas, from across the sea

150 **A una brazada**
At arm's length

151 **A una voz**
Unanimously

152 **A un tiempo**
At one (the same) time

153 **A veces**
At times

154 **A ver (si)**
Let's see (if)

155 **A vista de**
Within view, in presence of

156 **A vistas**
On approval

157 **A vuelo de pájaro**
As the crow flies

158 **A vuelta de correo**
By return mail

159 **Abogado de mala causa**
Devil's advocate

160 **Abrir paso para**
To make way for

161 **Acabar de (+inf.)**
To have just (done
something)

162 **Acabar por (+inf.)**
To end up by (doing
something)

163 **Acerca de**
About, with regard to

164 **Acordar con**
To be on good terms with

165 **¿Adónde va?**
Where are you going?

166 **Adondequiera que**
Wherever

167 **Agente viajero**
Traveling salesman

168 **Aglomeración de transeúntes** (or **automóviles**)
Traffic jam

169 **Agua cruda** (or **Agua pesada**)
Hard water

170 **Agua de manantial**
Spring water

171 **Agua de mar**
Sea (or salt) water

172 **Agua delgada**
Soft water

173 **Agua dulce**
Fresh (or soft) water

174 **Agua fina**
Soft water

175 **Agua potable**
Drinkable water, potable water

176 **Agua salada**
Salt water

177 **Aguantar el chubasco**
To weather the storm

178 **Aguas abajo**
Downstream

179 **Aguas arriba**
Upstream

180 **Aguas inmundas** (or **Aguas negras**)
Sewage

*181 **Águila o pico**
Heads or tails

*182 **Águila o sello**
Heads or tails

183 **Aguzar las orejas**
To prick up one's ears

184 **¡Ahí está el detalle!**
That's the point!

185 **Ahora bien**
Now then, well now, however

186 **Ahora es cuando.**
Now is the time. Now is your chance.

187 **Ahora mismo**
Right now, at once

188 **Ajustado a la ley**
In accordance with the law

189 **Al (+ inf.)**
On doing something

190 **Al aire libre**
In the open air

191 **Al amanecer**
At dawn, daybreak

192 **Al anochecer**
At dusk, nightfall

193 **Al azar**
By chance, at random

194 **Al cabo (de)**
Finally or after

195 **Al caer de la noche**
At nightfall

196 **Al centavo**
Just right, to the hair

197 **Al contado**
Cash

198 **Al contrario**
On the contrary

199 **Al cuidado de**
In care of

*200 **Al chas chas**
Cash down, cash and carry

201 **Al derecho**
Right side out

202 **Al (or En) derredor**
Around

203 **Al descubierto**
Openly

204 **Al detalle**
At retail

205 **Al día**
Per day

206 **Al día siguiente**
On the following day

207 **Al fiado**
On credit

208 **Al filo de - - - (las cinco)**
At about 5 o'clock

209 **Al fin**
At the end, at last

*210 **Al fin de cuentas**
In any case

*211 **Al fin y al cabo**
In short, at last, anyway

212 **Al frente de**
In front of

213 **Al habla**
Within speaking distance, in communication with

214 **Al igual**
Equally

215 **Al instante**
At once

216 **Al lado (de)**
At one's side, near at hand, next to

217 **Al mayoreo**
At wholesale

218 **Al menos (or A lo menos)**
At least, at the least

219 **Al menudeo (or Al por menor)**
At retail, in small quantities

220 **Al mismo tiempo**
At the same time

221 **Al oído**
Confidentially

222 **Al otro día**
On the following day

223 **Al otro lado de**
On the other side of

224 **Al pan, pan: al vino, vino.**
Call a spade a spade.

225 **Al pardear**
At twilight

226 **Al parecer**
Apparently

227 **Al pelo**
Perfectly, agreed, just right

228 **Al pie de la letra**
Literally

229 **Al (or A) poco rato**
In a short while, soon after

230 **Al presente**
Now, at present

231 **Al principio**
At first

232 **Al punto**
At once

233 **Al raso**
In the open air

234 **Al (or En) rededor**
Around, about

235 **Al remo**
At the oar, at hard labor

236 **Al revés**
Backwards, wrong side out, in the opposite way

237 **Al sereno**
In the night air

238 **Al sesgo**
On the bias, diagonally, obliquely

239 **Al soslayo**
On the bias, slanting,
obliquely

240 **Al tanteo**
Hit or miss, by guess

241 **Al través de**
Through, throughout

*242 **Al trote**
Quickly

243 **Al uso de la época**
According to the customs of
the period

244 **Alfiler de seguridad**
Safety pin²

245 **Algo por el estilo**
Similar, something of the sort

246 **Algo sordo**
Hard of hearing

247 **Algo tarde**
Rather late

248 **Algún día**
Sometime

249 **Algún otro**
Somebody else, some other

250 **Algún tiempo**
Sometime

251 **Alguna vez**
Sometime

252 **Algunas veces**
Sometimes

253 **Alondra de los prados**
Meadowlark

254 **Alquiler de**
For rent, for hire

255 **Alrededor de**
Around about, more or less

*256 **Alzar el codo**
To drink too much

*257 **Allá a las quinientas**
Once in a blue moon

258 **Allende el mar**
Across the sea, overseas

259 **¡Allí está el toque!**
There is the difficulty!

260 **Amante de**
Fond of

261 **Amigo de**
Fond of (friend of)

262 **Amor propio**
Self-esteem, pride, vanity

263 **Andar a gatas**
To creep, crawl

264 **Andar agitado**
To be out of sorts

265 **Andar bien**
To keep good time (e.g., a
watch), to work well, to be
right

266 **Andar (or Ir) de parranda**
To go on a spree

267 **Andarse con rodeos**
To beat around the bush

268 **Andarse el tiempo**
Meantime, as time goes on

269 **Andarse por las ramas**
To beat around the bush

270 **Andar tras los huesos de**
To chase after a woman

271 **Angina de pecho**
Angina pectoris

272 **Ante todo**
Especially, first of all, above
all

273 **Anteojos de larga vista**
Field glasses

274 **Antes de que**
Before

---

² or **el seguro**

275 **Antes que**
Rather than

276 **Año antepasado**
Year before last

277 **Año entrante**
Next year

278 **Año bisiesto**
Leap year

279 **Aparato auditivo**
Hearing aid

280 **Aparatos de pescar**
Fishing tackle

281 **Aparte de eso**
Besides that, aside from that

282 **Aprender de memoria**
To learn by heart

283 **Aprendiz de todo y oficial de nada**
Jack of all trades

284 **Aprovechar la ocasión**
To take advantage of the situation

285 **Aquí cerca**
Around (near) here

286 **Aquí mismo**
Right here

287 **Arco iris**
Rainbow

288 **Arranque automático**
Self-starter

289 **Arrebato (or Arranque) de cólera**
Fit of anger

290 **Así así**
So-so

291 **Así como**
Just as, the same as, as well as

292 **Así de largo**
That long

293 **Así es que**
So that, as soon as

294 **Así está bien.**
This will do (be O.K.).

295 **Así nada más**
Just plain, just as is

296 **Así pues**
So then, therefore

297 **Así que**
So that, as soon as, so, therefore

298 **¡Así se hace!**
Well done!, Bully for you!

299 **Así y todo**
In spite of that, even so, anyhow

300 **Ataque al corazón**
Heart failure

301 **Ataque cardíaco**
Heart attack

302 **Atracción sexual**
Sex appeal

303 **Atrás de**
Behind, in back of

304 **Aun así**
Even so

305 **Aun cuando**
Even if, even though

306 **Aún no**
Not yet

307 **Ave canora (or Ave cantora)**
Song bird

308 **Ave de rapiña**
Bird of prey

309 **Aventura amorosa**
Love affair

310 **Avión de reacción**
Jet airplane

311 **Avisos de ocasión**
Want ads

312 Ayer mismo
Just yesterday

313 Ayer por la tarde
Yesterday afternoon

B

*1 Bailar a secas
To dance without music

2 Baja el radio
Turn down the radio

*3 Bajo techo
Indoors

*4 Barrios bajos
Slums

*5 Batería de cocina
Set of kitchen utensils

6 Beber a pulso
To gulp down

7 Bien arreglada
Neatly dressed

8 Bien asado
Well-done (well-cooked)

9 Bien cocido
Well-done (well-cooked)

10 Bien me lo merezco
It serves me right

11 Bien parecido
Good-looking

12 Bien pienado
Well-groomed, trim

13 Bien que
Although

14 Bienes inmuebles
Real estate

15 Bienes muebles
Chattels, movable possessions

*16 Bienes raíces
Real estate

17 Billete de ida y vuelta
Round-trip ticket

18 Bobina distribuidora
Feed reel

19 Bobina receptora
Rewind or take-up reel

*20 Boca abajo
Face down, prone

*21 Boca arriba
Face up, supine

22 Boca calle
Side street (**bocacalle** = street intersection)

23 Boca de agua para incendios
Fireplug

24 Bomba atómica
Atomic bomb

25 Bomba de hidrógeno
Hydrogen bomb

26 Bote de salvamento
Life boat

27 Botón eléctrico
Push button

28 Broche de presión
Snap fastener

29 Bromas aparte
All joking aside

30 Buen mozo
Handsome man

31 ¡Buen provecho!
Good appetite! Enjoy your meal!

32 Buen rato
Pleasant (or long) time

33 Buen tipo
Good fellow

34 Buenas noches (tardes).
Good night (afternoon).

35 Buenos días.
Good morning. Good day.

36 **Buque pesquero**
Fishing boat

37 **Buque velero**
Sailboat

38 **Burlarse de**
To make fun of

C

1 **Caballo de raza**
Thoroughbred horse

2 **Cabeza de playa**
Beachhead

3 **Cabeza de puente**
Bridgehead

4 **Cabeza sonora**
Recording head

5 **Cada cual** (or **Cada uno**)
Each one

6 **¿Cada cuánto tiempo?**
How often?

7 **Cada dos días**
Every other day

8 **Cada uno**
Apiece

9 **Cada vez menos**
Less and less

10 **Caer bien**
To fit well, to be becoming, to please

11 **Caer mal**
To fit badly, displease

*12 **Caer en cama**
To fall ill

*13 **Caer en la cuenta**
To realize, to get the point

14 **Caer en gracia**
To please

*15 **Café solo**
Black coffee

16 **Caja de ahorros**
Savings bank

17 **Caja de cambios**
Automotive transmission

18 **Caja de seguridad**
Safe deposit box (in a bank)

19 **Caja fuerte**
A safe, strong box

20 **Caja registradora**
Cash register

21 **Cajón de muerto**
Coffin

*22 **Cajón de ropa**
Dry goods or clothing store

23 **Calculador electrónico**
Computer

*24 **Calentura de pollo**
Feigned illness

25 **Caliente de cascos**
Hot headed

*26 **¡Cállate la trompa!**
Shut up!

27 **Calle abajo**
Down the street

28 **Calle arriba**
Up the street

29 **Callejón sin salida**
Blind alley

30 **Cállese, por favor**
Please be quiet

31 **Cambiar de engrane** (or **velocidad**)
To shift gears

32 **Cambiar de idea** (or **pensamiento** or **opinión**)
To change one's mind

33 **Cambiar de marcha**
To shift gears

34 **Cambiar de tema**
To change the subject

*35 **Caminar con pies de plomo**
To go cautiously

36 **Camino carretero**
Highway

37 **Camino de**
On the way to, on the road to

38 **Camino real**
Highway[3] (the main route)

39 **Camino trillado**
Beaten path

40 **Camión de reparto**
Delivery truck

41 **Camisa de fuerza**
Straight jacket

42 **Campo de aterrizaje**
Landing field

*43 **Cara de hereje**
Hideous face

44 **Carbón de leña**
Charcoal

45 **Cargar con**
To carry away, assume responsibility

*46 **Cargar con el muerto**
To get the blame unjustly

47 **Cargar en cuenta**
To charge on account

48 **Carne de gallina**
"Goose flesh" or "goose pimples"

49 **Carne de res** (or **Carne de vaca**)
Beef

50 **Carpa dorada**
Goldfish

51 **Carrete distribuidor**
Feed reel

52 **Carrete receptor**
Take-up reel

53 **Carta blanca**
Full authority, freedom to act

54 **Carta de naturaleza**
Naturalization papers

55 **Carta de venta**
Bill of sale

56 **Casa de empeños**
Pawnshop

57 **Casa de huéspedes**
Boarding house

58 **Casa de locos**
Insane asylum

59 **Casa de moneda**
Mint (re money)

60 **Casa de socorro**
Emergency hospital

*61 **Casa de vecindad**
Tenement

62 **Casarse con**
To marry (someone)

63 **Casi nunca**
Hardly ever

64 **Castañetear con los dedos**
To snap one's fingers

65 **Catarro asmático**
Hay fever

66 **Cédula de vecindad** (or **Cédula de personal**)
Official identification card

67 **Cemento armado**
Reinforced concrete

68 **Cepillo de dientes**
Toothbrush

69 **Cerca de**
Near to, close to

70 **Cerrarse el cielo**
To become overcast, cloudy

71 **Certificado** (or **Fe**, or **Partida**) **de nacimiento**
Birth certificate

---

[3] or **la carretera**

72 **Cerveza de barril**
Draft beer

73 **Cerveza de jengibre**
Ginger ale

74 **Cifrar la esperanza en**
To place one's hope in

75 **Cinturón de seguridad**
Safety belt

76 **Clara de huevo**
White of an egg

77 **Claro que sí**
Of course, naturally

78 **Claro que no**
Of course not, certainly not

79 **Coche cama**
Sleeping car

80 **Coche comedor**
Dining car

81 **Coche salón**
Parlor car

82 **Coger catarro (or un resfriado)**
To catch cold

83 **Coger fuego**
To catch fire

84 **Col de bruselas**
Brussels sprouts

85 **Colmo de la locura**
Height of folly

*86 **Comer a deshora**
To piece between meals

87 **Comercio exterior**
Foreign trade

88 **Como a costumbre**
At about

89 **Como de costumbre**
As usual

90 **Como dijo el otro**
As someone said

*91 **Como Dios manda**
According to Hoyle (the rules)

92 **Como en**
In about

93 **¿Cómo le va?**
How are you?

94 **Como mínimo**
At least

95 **Como no**
Unless

96 **¿Cómo no?**
Of course, why not?

97 **Como que**
Since, inasmuch as

98 **Como quiera que**
Since, inasmuch as

99 **Como quiera que sea**
At any rate

100 **¿Cómo se dice?**
How do you say - - -?

101 **¿Cómo se llama Ud.?**
What is your name?

102 **¿Cómo se vende?**
How is it sold? How much is it?

103 **Como si**
As if

104 **Como si tal cosa**
Serene, as if nothing had happened

105 **Como si fuera**
As if it were

106 **Como siempre**
As usual, like always

107 **Como sigue**
As follows

108 **Como último recurso**
As a last resort

109 **Como una seda**
Soft as silk, smoothly, sweet-tempered

*110 **Como visita de obispo**
Once in a blue moon

111 **Compota de manzana**
Applesauce

112 **Con anticipación**
In advance

113 **Con delirio**
Madly

114 **Con el propósito de**
With the aim of

115 **Con (or En or Por) extremo**
Very much, extremely

116 **Con fuerzas para - (la tarea)**
Equal to - (the task)

117 **Con la corriente**
Down stream

*118 **Con la lengua de corbata (or Con la lengua de pechera)**
Out of breath, with tongue hanging out

119 **Con motivo de**
With the idea of, because of, on occasion of, on account of

120 **Con mucha frequencia**
Frequently, very often[4]

121 **Con mucho gusto**
Gladly, willingly

122 **Con permiso**
Excuse me, with your permission

*123 **¿Con qué cara?**
How can I (one) have the nerve?

124 **¡Con razón!**
No wonder!

125 **Con respecto a**
With regard to

126 **Con rumbo a**
In the direction of

127 **Con somnolencia**
Sleepily

128 **Con tal (de) que**
Provided that, so that

129 **Con tiempo**
In advance, in good time

130 **Con todo (or Con todos los obstáculos)**
In spite of that

131 **Conciliar el sueño**
To get to sleep

132 **Confiar en**
To trust, rely on

133 **Conforme a**
In accordance with

134 **Congreso (or Cámara) de Diputados**
House of Representatives

135 **Conocer de vista**
To know by sight

136 **Consigo mismo**
To oneself

137 **Conspirar contra una persona**
To frame someone

138 **Consultarlo con la almohada**
To sleep on it

139 **Contar con**
To reckon with, rely on, count on

140 **Contra la corriente**
Up stream

*141 **Contra viento y marea**
Against all odds

---

[4] or **frequentamente** or **a menudo**

142 **Contraer matrimonio**
To get married

143 **Contraseña de salida**
Theatre stub (or check) for
re-entry

144 **Control de natalidad**
Birth control

145 **Convenirle a uno**
To be to one's advantage

146 **Correo aéreo**
Air mail

147 **Correr por cuenta de uno**
To be one's own affair, to be
up to oneself

148 **Correr riesgo**
To take a chance, to risk

149 **Corrida de toros**
Bullfight

150 **Corrida del tiempo**
Swiftness of time

151 **Cortadora de césped**
Lawnmower

152 **Cortar el hilo**
To break the thread of a story,
to interrupt

153 **Corto de oído**
Hard of hearing

154 **Corto de vista**
Nearsighted

155 **Cosa de**
Approximately, about[5]

156 **Costar trabajo**
To be very difficult

157 **Creer que no**
To think not

158 **Creer que sí**
To think so

159 **Cruzarse con**
To meet

160 **Cuajado de**
Full of, or covered with

161 **¿Cuál es cuál?**
Which is which?

162 **¿Cuál es el precio?**
How much is it?

163 **Cualquier cosa**
Anything at all

164 **Cualquiera** (or
Cualesquiera) de los dos
Either of the two

165 **Cuando quiera**
Whenever

166 **Cuanto antes**
As soon as possible

167 **¿Cuánto le cabe?**
How much does it hold?

168 **¿Cuánto tiempo hace?**
How long ago?

169 **Cuarto de baño**
Bathroom

170 **Cuatro letras**
A few lines

171 **Cuatro palabras**
A few words

172 **Cuenta abierta**
Charge account

173 **Cuenta de crédito**
Charge account

174 **Cuenta en común**
Joint account

*175 **Cuento chino**
Cock and bull story

176 **Cuero de vaca**
Cowhide

177 **Cuerpo docente**
Faculty of a school

178 **Cuesta abajo**
Downhill

---

[5] or **aproximadamente** or **casi**

179 **Cuesta arriba**
Uphill

180 **Cueste lo que cueste**
At any cost

*181 **Cumplir años**
To have a birthday

182 **Cumplir su palabra**
To keep one's word

183 **Cuota de entrada**
Admission fee

CH

1 **Cheque de viajero**
Traveler's check

2 **Chueco o derecho**
Hit or miss, happy-go-lucky

D

1 **Dado caso**
Supposing

2 **Dado el caso que**
Provided that

3 **Dar a**
To face, look towards, give to

4 **Dar a conocer**
To make known

5 **Dar a crédito**
To loan on credit

6 **Dar a entender**
To pretend

*7 **Dar a luz**
To give birth, to publish

8 **Dar al traste con**
To ruin, destroy

9 **Dar al través con**
To ruin, destroy

10 **Dar ánimo**
To cheer up

11 **Dar atención**
To pay attention

12 **Dar batería**
To raise a rumpus, to work hard

13 **Dar calabazas**
To reject, to jilt

14 **Dar caza**
To pursue, track down

15 **Dar cima**
To complete, carry out

16 **Dar coba**
To flatter, tease

17 **Dar cuenta de**
To give a report on

18 **Dar cuerda a**
To wind (a watch)

19 **Dar de alta**
To discharge (a patient)

20 **Dar de baja**
To dismiss, or kick out

21 **Dar de comer**
To feed, be fed

22 **Dar disgustos a**
To cause distress or grief to

23 **Dar el pecho**
To nurse (a baby)

24 **Dar el pésame por**
To extend condolences to or for

25 **Dar el visto bueno**
To approve, O.K.

26 **Dar en**
To hit or to hit upon

27 **Dar en cara**
To reproach, blame

28 **Dar en el clavo**
To hit the nail on the head

29 **Dar en tierra con alguien**
To overthrow someone

30 **Dar en** (or **Dar con**) **el chiste**
To guess right, hit the nail on the head

*31 **Dar esquinazo**
To "ditch", avoid meeting someone

32 **Dar fe de**
To vouch for

33 **Dar fin (a)**
To complete

*34 **Dar gato por liebre**
To cheat or swindle

*35 **Dar grasa**
To polish (shoes)

36 **Dar guerra**
To make trouble

37 **Dar gusto**
To please

38 **Dar horror**
To frighten, horrify

39 **Dar jabón (a)**
To "soft soap" (flatter) a person

40 **Dar la bienvenida**
To welcome

41 **Dar las espaldas a**
To turn one's back on

42 **Dar la hora**
To strike the hour

*43 **Dar la lata**
To annoy

44 **Dar la mano**
To help, shake hands

45 **Dar la noticia**
To break the news

46 **Dar la razón**
To agree, to be of same opinion

47 **Dar la razón a una persona**
To admit a person is right

48 **Dar** (or **Darse**) **la vuelta**
To turn (to turn around)

49 **Dar largas**
To postpone or delay, or give someone the run around

50 **Dar las gracias**
To give thanks, to thank

51 **Dar lástima (de)**
To arouse pity or sorrow

52 **Dar lo mismo**
To make no difference

53 **Dar los recuerdos**
To give regards

54 **Dar lugar a**
To give cause for

55 **Dar lustre**
To polish

56 **Dar marcha atrás**
To back up

57 **Dar mucha pena**
To cause sorrow, to be disconcerting

58 **Dar parte**
To inform

59 **Dar pie**
To give opportunity (or occasion to)

60 **Dar por**
To consider as

61 **Dar por descontado**
To take for granted

62 **Dar por hecho**
To take for granted, to consider as done

63 **Dar por sabido**
To take for granted

64 **Dar por sentado**
To take for granted

65 **Dar por supuesto**
To take for granted

66 **Dar prestado**
To lend

67 **Dar propina**
To tip (give a gratuity)

68 **Dar que hacer**
To cause extra work

69 **Dar rabia**
To anger

70 **Dar razón**
To inform, give account

71 **Dar realce**
To enhance, emphasize

72 **Dar sepultura**
To bury

73 **Dar un paseo**
To take a walk or ride

74 **Dar un paseo por mar**
To go for a sail

75 **Dar un paso**
To take a step

76 **Dar un pisotón**
To step hard upon

77 **Dar un portazo**
To slam the door

78 **Dar un salto (or Dar saltos)**
To leap, jump

79 **Dar un traspié**
To trip, stumble

80 **Dar un vistazo a**
To glance over, peruse

81 **Dar una cita**
To make an appointment

82 **Dar una fiesta**
To give (throw) a party

83 **Dar una pasada por**
To pass by, walk by

84 **Dar una pisada**
To step (stomp) on (upon)

85 **Dar una satisfacción**
To apologize

86 **Dar una vuelta**
To take a stroll

*87 **Dar uno en la tecla**
To hit the nail on the head, find the right way to do something

*88 **Darle a uno mala espina**
To arouse one's suspicion

89 **Darle lo mismo.**
It makes no difference.

90 **Darle vuelta a la hoja**
To turn the page

91 **Darlo por abandonado**
To give it up

92 **Darse calabazas**
To fail, to be jilted, to be rejected

93 **Darse cuenta de (que)**
To realize (that), to notice

94 **Darse de baja**
To drop out

95 **Darse farol**
To show off, put on airs

96 **Darse la mano**
To shake hands

97 **Darse por vencido (or Me doy)**
To give up, (I give up)

98 **Darse prisa**
To hurry

99 **Darse tono**
To put on airs

100 **Darse un tropezón**
To trip, stumble

101 **Darse un encontrón**
To collide with, bump into each other

102 **Darse un resbalón**
To slip

103 **Dárselas de**
To pose as

104 **De acuerdo con**
In accordance with

105 **De ahí en adelante**
From then on

106 **De ahora en adelante**
From now on, in the future

107 **De algún modo**
Somehow

108 **De algún tiempo para acá**
For sometime now

109 **De alguna manera**
Somehow

110 **De arriba abajo**
From top to bottom

111 **De aquel tiempo en adelante**
From that time on

112 **De aquí en adelante**
From now on

113 **De aquí para allá**
To and fro, back and forth

114 **De balde**
Free of charge, gratis

*115 **De bote en bote**
Crowded

116 **De bracete**
Arm in arm

117 **De broma**
Jokingly, in jest

118 **De buen tomo y lomo**
Bulky, important

119 **De buen tono**
In good taste, stylish

120 **De buen ver**
Good-looking

121 **De buena cepa**
Of good stock

122 **De buena fe**
In good faith

123 **De buena gana (or De buen grado)**
Willingly, gladly

124 **De buena ley**
Of good quality

125 **De buenas a primeras**
All of a sudden, unexpectedly, on the spur of the moment

126 **De burla**
In jest

127 **De cabo a rabo**
From beginning to end

128 **De camino (or De camino real)**
On the way

129 **De canto**
On edge

130 **De copete**
High rank, important, proud

131 **De corrida**
Without stopping

132 **De cualquier modo**
At any rate

133 **De cuando en cuando**
Sometimes, occasionally

134 **De día**
By day, before dark

135 **De dientes afuera**
Insincerely

136 **¡De dónde!**
Nonsense!

137 **De dos caras**
Two-faced

138 **De dos en dos**
By twos, two by two

139 **De dos sentidos**
Two-way

140 **De ese modo (or De esa manera)**
In that way

141 **De espaldas**
On one's back, supine

142 **De este modo** (or **De esta manera**)
In this way

143 **De etiqueta**
Formal

144 **De golpe**
Suddenly

145 **De gorra**
At another's expense

146 **De grado en grado**
By degrees

147 **De hecho**
In fact

148 **De hilo**[6]
Without stopping

149 **De hoy en adelante**
From now on

150 **De hoy en ocho días**
One week from today

151 **De hoy en quince días**
Two weeks from today

152 **De improviso**
Unexpectedly

153 **De la noche a la mañana**
Overnight

154 **De lado**
Tilted, oblique, sideways

155 **De lejos**
From a distance

156 **De lo contrario**
If not, otherwise

157 **De lo lindo**
Wonderfully, very much, to the utmost

158 **De mal en peor**
From bad to worse

159 **De mal grado**
Reluctantly, unwillingly

160 **De mal gusto**
In poor taste

161 **De mal temple**
In a bad humor

162 **De mala fe**
In bad faith, deceitfully

163 **De mala gana**
Unwillingly

164 **De mala suerte**
Unlucky

165 **De manera que**
So that

166 **De marca**
Of excellent quality

167 **De mayor venta**
Best seller

168 **De mejor agrado**
With great pleasure

169 **De memoria**
By heart

170 **De moda**
In vogue, stylish

171 **De modo que**
So what?, so that, and so

172 **De momento**
For the time being

173 **De nada.**
Don't mention it. You're welcome.

174 **De ningún modo**
By no means

---

[6] Choice of prepositions used with "**hilo**" may vary locally. Reference No. 9 (APP. B) gives these meanings:

a hilo = without interruption
al hilo = along the thread
de hilo = straight, without stopping

175 **¡De ninguna manera!**
By no means!, I should say not!

176 **De noche**
By (at) night

177 **De nuevo**
Again, once again

178 **De ocasión**
Reduced price, a bargain

179 **De (or Al) oído**
By ear

180 **De oídos**
Rumor, hearsay

181 **De ordinario**
Ordinary, usual

182 **De otro modo**
Otherwise

183 **De palabra**
By word of mouth

184 **De par en par**
Wide open

185 **De parte a parte**
Through, from one side to the other

186 **De parte de**
On behalf of, in favor of

187 **¿De parte de quién?**
Who is calling?

188 **De paso**
In passing, at the same time, by the way, in transit

189 **De perlas**
Perfectly, to the point

190 **De pie**
Standing

191 **De pilón**
To boot, besides, in addition

192 **De poca monta**
Of little value or importance

193 **De poquito**
In small amounts

194 **De por sí**
Separately, by itself

195 **De prisa**
Quickly

196 **De pronto**
At once, suddenly

197 **De propósito**
On purpose

198 **De punta**
On end

199 **De puntillas (or De puntas)**
On tiptoes

200 **De punto**
Knitted, by the minute

201 **De pura casualidad**
By pure chance

202 **¿De qué se trata?**
What is it about? What does it deal with?

203 **¿De qué tamaño es?**
What size is it?

204 **De raíz**
By the roots, completely

205 **De rebote**
On the rebound, indirectly

206 **De relieve**
In relief, outstanding, prominent

207 **De remate**
Absolutely, without remedy

208 **De repente**
Suddenly, all of a sudden

209 **De repuesto**
Spare, extra

210 **De resultas**
As a result, consequently

211 **De rigor**
A "must", It must

212 **De rodillas**
On one's knees

213 De seguida
Continuously, without interruption

214 De segunda mano
Second hand

215 De seguro
For certain, for sure

216 De sobra
More than enough, unnecessary

217 De sol a sol
Sunrise to sunset

218 De soslayo
Slanting, sideways

219 De subida
On the way up

220 De súbito
Suddenly

221 De suerte que
So that, and so, in such a way

222 De suyo
Naturally, by nature

223 De tarde en tarde
From time to time, now and then, once in a blue moon

224 De tejas abajo
Here below, in this world

225 De todas maneras
Anyway, at any rate

226 De todos modos
At any rate, in any case, anyhow, by all means

227 De tránsito
In transit, on the way, passing through

228 De través
Across

229 De un golpe
All at once

230 De un modo u otro
Somehow, in some way or other

231 De un momento a otro
At any moment

232 De un salto
Quickly

233 De un solo sentido
One way (e.g., a one-way street)

234 De un tirón
All at once, with a big pull

235 De una pieza
Solid, of one piece

236 De una tirada
All at once, in one fell swoop

237 De una vez
At once, at one time, at one stroke, once and for all

238 De una vez por todas
Once and for all

239 De uno en uno
One at a time

240 De unos
Of about

241 De uso
Second hand

242 De vacaciones
On vacation

243 De venta
On sale

244 De veras (¿De veras?)
Really, in truth, in earnest, (Really? Is that so?)

245 De verdad (¿De verdad?)
Truly, truthfully, (Really?, Is that so?)

246 De vez en cuando
Now and then, occasionally

247 De vicio
As a (bad) habit

248 De viva voz
By word of mouth

249 **De (buena) voluntad**
Willingly, with pleasure

250 **De vuelta**
Again

251 **Debajo de**
Under, beneath

252 **Debe de ser**
It must be, it probably is

253 **Decir para sí**
To say to one's self

*254 **Decir para su coleto** (or **capote**)
To say to one's self

255 **Dedo del corazón**
Middle finger

256 **Dedo del pie**
Toe

257 **Dedo meñique**
Little finger

258 **Dedo pulgar**
Thumb

259 **Dejar a uno plantado**
To "stand someone up"

260 **Dejar caer**
To drop

261 **Dejar de** (+ _inf._)
To stop - - -

262 **Dejar de asistir**
To drop out

263 **Dejar dicho**
To leave word

264 **Dejar en paz**
To let be, to leave alone

265 **Dejar saber**
To let on, pretend

266 **Dejar tranquilo**
To leave alone

267 **Dejarse de cuentos**.
Come to the point. Stop beating around the bush.

268 **Dejarse de rodeos**.
Stop the excuses. Stop beating around the bush.

269 **Déjeme salir**
Let me out

270 **Del mismo modo**
Of the same sort, in the same way

271 **Del natural**
From nature, from life (e.g., a painting)

272 **Del próximo pasado**
Of last month

273 **Del todo**
Wholly, at all

274 **Delante de**
In front of

275 **Dentro de**
Inside of, within

276 **Dentro de poco**
In a little while

277 **Dentro de un momento**
In a short time

278 **Dentro de una semana**
Within a week

279 **Depósito de maderas**
Lumber yard

280 **Derechos de autor**
Copyright

281 **Derramamiento de sangre**
Bloodshed

*282 **Desayunarse con la noticia**
To hear a piece of news early or for the first time

283 **Descabezar el sueño**
To take a nap

284 **Desde ahora**
From now on

285 **Desde el principio**
All along, from the beginning

286 **Desde entonces**
Since then, ever since

287 **Desde hace**
Dating from, over a period
of - - -

288 **Desde lejos**
From a distance, from afar

289 **Desde luego**
Actually, of course, at once

290 **Desde que**
Since

291 **Desde un principio**
From the beginning

292 **Desempeñar un papel**
To play a part

293 **Despedirse de**
To say goodbye to

294 **Después de eso**
Thereafter

295 **Después de todo**
After all

296 **Desviarse hacia la derecha**
To pull over to the right

297 **Detrás de**
Behind, in back of

298 **Devanarse los sesos**
To rack one's brain

299 **Día de campo**
Picnic

*300 **Día de raya**
Payday

301 **Día de semana** (or **Día de trabajo**)
Weekday

302 **Día del juicio final**
Judgment day

303 **Día festivo**
Holiday

304 **Día hábil**
Weekday, workday

305 **Día tras día**
Day after day

306 **Días de antaño**
Days of old

307 **Días de semana**
Weekdays

308 **Dicho y hecho**
Sure enough, no sooner said
than done

309 **Diente de león**
Dandelion

310 **Dificultar el paso**
To obstruct, impede

311 **Digno de**
Well worth it

312 **Digno de confianza**
Reliable, trustworthy

313 **Dinero contante y sonante**
Ready (or hard) cash

314 **Dinero menudo**
Change (re money)

315 **Dios mediante**
God willing

316 **Dique de construcción** (or **Dique de carenar**)
Dry dock

317 **Dique flotante**
Floating dock

318 **Disculpa pobre**
Lame excuse

319 **Disminuir el volumen**
To turn down the volume

320 **Doblar la esquina** (or **calle**)
To turn the corner

321 **Docena cabal**
Even dozen

322 **Dolerle a uno la garganta**
To have a sore throat

323 **Dolor de cabeza**
Headache

324 **Dolor de muelas**
Toothache

325 **Donde no**
Otherwise, if not

326 **Dondequiera que (or Por dondequiera que)**
Wherever

327 **Dormir a pierna suelta**
To sleep soundly

*328 **Dormir la mona**
To sleep it off

329 **Dormir la siesta**
To take an afternoon nap

E

1 **Echar a correr (or Echarse a correr)**
To begin running (to run away)

2 **Echar(se) a perder**
To spoil, to ruin

3 **Echar a pique**
To sink

4 **Echar al correo**
To mail, to post

5 **Echar al olvido**
To forget on purpose

6 **Echar carnes**
To put on weight, get fat

7 **Echar de menos**
To miss

8 **Echar de ver**
To notice, to observe

9 **Echar en (or Dar en) cara**
To reproach, blame

10 **Echar espumarajos**
To froth at the mouth, to be very angry

11 **Echar flores**
To throw bouquets, to flatter, to compliment

*12 **Echar la casa por la ventana**
To spare no expense, squander everything

13 **Echar la culpa a**
To blame

14 **Echar la garra**
To arrest, grab

*15 **Echar la llave**
To lock the door

*16 **Echar la uña**
To steal

17 **Echar la zarpa**
To grasp, to seize

18 **Echar leva**
To draft, conscript

19 **Echar mano**
To seize

20 **Echar pajas**
To draw lots

*21 **Echar papas**
To fib

22 **Echar por tierra**
To knock down, demolish

23 **Echar raíces**
To take root, become firmly fixed

24 **Echar suertes**
To draw lots

25 **Echar un piropo**
To compliment, flatter

26 **Echar un sueño**
To take a nap

27 **Echar (or Soltar) un terno**
To say a bad word, to swear, curse

28 **Echar un trago**
To take a drink

*29 Echar una cana al aire
To go out for a good time or
fling

30 Echar una carta al correo
To mail a letter

31 Echar una siesta
To take a nap

***32 Echarle la bendición a una
cosa**
To give something up for lost

33 Echarse a
To begin to (do something)

34 Echarse al coleto
To drink down, devour

35 Echarse atrás
To back out, to go back on
one's word

36 Efusión de sangre
Bloodshed

37 Ejecutor de la justicia
Executioner

38 El año (or El mes) entrante
Next year (or month)

39 El año (or El mes) pasado
Last year (or month)

**40 El año (or El mes) que
viene**
Next year (or month)

41 El caso es
The fact is

42 El común de las gentes
The majority of the people,
the average person

43 El cuento del tío
Deceitful story told to get
money

44 El de
The one with

45 El día menos pensado
When least expected,
unexpectedly

46 El está por hacerlo
He is in favor of doing it

47 El fin de semana
Weekend

48 El gusto es mío
The pleasure is mine

49 El más reciente
The latter

50 El mismísimo hombre
The very man

**51 El mismo que (or Lo mismo
que)**
The same as

52 El pro y el contra
Pro and con

53 El que
The one who, the one which

54 El sol poniente
The setting sun

**55 El tren llegó con (x)
minutos de retraso**
The train was (x) minutes
late

56 El uno al otro
Each other

**57 El uno o el otro (or Uno u
otro)**
Either, one or the other

58 Empeñar la palabra
To promise, pledge

59 Empinar el codo
To drink (too much)

60 En abonos
On installments

61 En absoluto
Absolutely (<u>not</u>)

62 En adelante
In future, from now on

63 En alguna otra parte
Somewhere else

64 **En alguna parte**
Somewhere

65 **En ambos casos**
In either case

66 **En aquel tiempo**
At that time, in those days

*67 **En balde**
In vain

68 **En breve**
Shortly

69 **En broma**
In jest, as a joke

70 **En buen romance**
In plain language

71 **En cambio**
On the other hand

72 **En casa**
At home, indoors

73 **En caso afirmativo**
If so

74 **En caso de**
In the event of

75 **En caso de que**
In case of (that)

76 **En concreto**
Concretely, to sum up

77 **En conformidad con**
In compliance with

78 **En conjunto**
As a whole

79 **En contra de**
Against, opposed to

80 **En cualquier caso**
Anyway

81 **En cuanto**
As soon as

82 **En cuanto a**
As for, with regard to

83 **En cueros**
Naked

84 **En cuerpo**
Hatless and coatless

85 **En curso**
In progress

86 **En descubierto**
Uncovered, unpaid

87 **En días pasados**
In days gone by

88 **En efecto**
In fact, indeed, really

89 **En el acto**
Right away, at once

90 **En el extranjero**
Abroad, out of the country

91 **En el fondo**
At bottom, at heart, in
substance

92 **En el momento preciso**
In the nick of time

*93 **En el quinto infierno**
Very far away

94 **En el sigilo de la noche**
In the dead of the night

95 **En especial**
Especially, in particular

96 **En espera de**
Awaiting

97 **En estado interesante**
Pregnant

98 **En existencia**
In stock, on hand

99 **En fecha a próxima**
At an early date

100 **En fin**
In short, finally, in
conclusion

101 **En fragante**
In the act

102 **En grande**
On a large scale

103 **En grueso**
In bulk, by wholesale

104 **En junto (or En conjunto)**
All together, in all

105 **En la actualidad**
At the present time

106 **En libertad**
Free

107 **En lo futuro**
In the future

108 **En lo más crudo del invierno**
In the dead of winter

109 **En lo sucesivo**
Hereafter, in future

110 **En lontananza**
In the distance, in the background

111 **En lugar de**
Instead of, in place of

112 **En manga de camisa**
In shirt sleeves

113 **En marcha**
In progress

114 **En muchos puntos**
In many respects

115 **En (or Al) ninguna parte**
Nowhere

116 **En obsequio de**
In honor of, for the sake of

117 **En observación**
Under observation

118 **En otros términos**
In other words

119 **En parte**
Partly

120 **En particular**
Especially

121 **En pleno día**
In broad daylight

122 **En pleno rostro (or En plana cara)**
Right on the face

123 **En poder de**
In the hands of

124 **En prenda de**
As proof of, as a pledge

125 **En pro de**
On behalf of

126 **En pro y en contra**
For and against

127 **En punto**
On the dot, sharp

128 **¿En qué puedo servirle?**
What can I do for you?

129 **En rama**
Crude

130 **En realidad**
As a matter of fact

131 **En regla**
In order

132 **En resolución**
In brief

133 **En resumen**
Summing up, in brief

134 **En resumidas cuentas**
In short, after all

135 **En rigor**
In fact, in reality

136 **En rueda**
In turn, in a circle

137 **En (or A la) rústica**
Unbound, paper bound

138 **En salvo**
In safety, out of danger

139 **En sazón**
Ripe, in season, opportunely

140 **En secreto**
Secretly

141 **En seguida**
At once, right now

142 **En señal de**
In proof of, in token of

143 **En serio**
Seriously

144 **En sueños**
In one's sleep

145 **En tal caso**
In such a case

146 **En tanto que**
While

147 **En todas partes**
Everywhere

148 **En todo caso**
In any event

149 **En un credo**
In a jiffy, in a minute

*150 **En un chiflido**
In a jiffy, in a second

151 **En un improviso**
In a moment

152 **En un salto**
Quickly

*153 **En un soplo**
In a jiffy, in a second

154 **En vela**
On watch, without sleep

155 **En verdad**
Really, truly

156 **En vez de**
Instead of

157 **En vigor**
In force, in effect

158 **En vista de que**
Since, in view of

159 **En voz alta**
Aloud, loud voice

160 **En voz baja**
In a low voice, whispering

161 **Enajenamiento de los sentidos**
Loss of consciousness

162 **Encargarse de**
To take charge of

163 **Encima de**
On, upon

164 **Encogerse de hombros**
To shrug one's shoulders

165 **Encontrarse con**
To come across, to meet

166 **Enfermedad de corazón**
Heart trouble

167 **Enfrentarse con**
To confront, meet face to face

168 **Enredarse con**
To have an affair with

169 **Entablar una conversación**
To start a conversation

170 **Entablar un pleito**
To bring a lawsuit

171 **Enteramente nuevo**
Brand new

172 **Entrar en vigor**
To become effective (e.g., law)

*173 **Entre azul y buenas noches**
Undecided, on the fence

174 **Entre bastidores**
Behind the scenes, off-stage

*175 **Entre la espada y la pared**
Between devil and deep blue sea

*176 **Entre paréntesis**
By the way

177 **Entre semana**
During the week

178 **Entre tanto**
Meanwhile, all the while, at the same time

179 **Equipo de novia**
Trousseau

180 **Error de imprenta**
Printing error

181 **Error de máquina**
Typing error

182 **Es cierto.**
It's true.

183 **Es decir**
That is to say

184 **Es (la) hora de (partir)**
It is time for, It is time to (go)

185 **Es lo de menos.**
It makes no difference.
That's the least of the trouble.

186 **Escoba mecánica**
Carpet sweeper

187 **Escribir a máquina**
To typewrite

188 **Escribir al dictado**
To take dictation

189 **Escrito a máquina**
Typewritten

190 **Eso corre prisa.**
That is urgent.

191 **Eso es.**
That is it, That's right.

192 **¡Eso es el colmo!**
That is the limit!

193 **Eso es harina de otro costal.**
That's a horse of a different color. (cf. SEC. III)

194 **Eso estriba en que**
The basis for it is that - - -

195 **Eso no tiene quite.**
That can't be helped.

196 **Eso sí.**
That was true.

197 **Espejo de cuerpo entero**
Full-length mirror

198 **Esperar en alguien**
To place hope (or confidence) in someone

199 **Esperar todo el santo día**
To wait the whole blessed day

200 **Espuma de jabón**
Suds

201 **Esquí náutico** (or **Esquí acuático**)
Water ski

202 **Está de más.**
It is unnecessary, superfluous.

203 **Está nublado.**
It is cloudy.

204 **Está por hacer.**
It is yet to be done.

205 **Estación de gasolina**
Gasoline station[7]

206 **Estamos a mano.**
We are even, quits.

207 **Estar a buen recaudo**
To be safe

208 **Estar a cargo de**
To be in charge of

209 **Estar a gusto**
To be contented or comfortable

210 **Estar a la mira de**
To be alert for, on the lookout for

211 **Estar a punto de**
To be about to

212 **Estar al cabo de**
To be well-informed, up-to-date

213 **Estar al corriente de**
To be informed, to be up-to-date

---

[7] or **la gasolinera**

214 **Estar afecto a**
To be fond of, to be prone to

215 **Estar afilando con** (or **Afilar con**)
To flirt with

216 **Estar arreglado**
To be in order

217 **Estar bien**
To be all right, O.K.
Ex: **Está bien.**
(It is) all right, (It's) O.K.

218 **Estar bien de salud**
To be in good health

219 **Estar bruja**
To be broke

220 **Estar con - - -**
To have - - - (an illness, discomfort, etc.)

221 **Estar con mucha pena**
To be very sorry

222 **Estar crudo**
To have a hangover

223 **Estar de acuerdo**
To agree

*224 **Estar de bote en bote**
To be crowded, be completely filled up

225 **Estar de conformidad con**
To be in compliance with

226 **Estar de duelo**
To mourn, be in mourning

*227 **Estar de goma**
To have a hangover

228 **Estar de luto**
To be in mourning

229 **Estar de malas**
To be out of luck

230 **Estar** (or **Quedar**) **de non**
To be left alone, without a partner or companion

231 **Estar de parto**
To be in labor

232 **Estar de paso**
To be passing through

233 **Estar de prisa**
To be in a hurry

234 **Estar de regreso**
To be back

235 **Estar de sobra**
To be in the way

236 **Estar de turno**
To be on duty

237 **Estar de vacaciones**
To be on vacation

238 **Estar de** (or **Estar en**) **vena**
To be in the mood

239 **Estar de venta**
To be on sale

240 **Estar de viaje**
To be traveling, on the road

241 **Estar de vuelta**
To be back

242 **Estar desahogado**
To be well-off

243 **Estar dispuesto**
To be willing

244 **Estar en el bote** (or **Estar en cana**)
To be in the jug (jail)

245 **Estar en buen uso**
To be in good condition (re a thing)

246 **Estar en camino**
To be on the way

247 **Estar en curso**
To be going on

248 **Estar en deuda con**
To be indebted to

249 **Estar en la buena boya**
To be in a good humor

250 Estar en las mismas
To be in the same boat

251 Estar en las nubes
To daydream

252 Estar en las últimas
To be on one's last legs, to be
at the end of one's rope, out
of resources

253 Estar en pañales
To be in infancy, to possess
scant knowledge

254 Estar en peligro
To be in danger

255 Estar en pugna con
To be opposed to, to be in
conflict with, to be against

256 Estar en sala de
To be waiting for, expecting

257 Estar en todo
To have a finger in everything

258 Estar en un aprieto
To be in a jam, to be in
trouble

259 Estar en un error
To be wrong, to be mistaken

260 Estar en vela
To be in the mood, inspired

261 Estar encargado de
To have charge of, to be in
charge of

262 Estar engranado
To be in gear

**263 Estar entre la espada y la
pared**
To be between the devil and
the deep blue sea (cf. SEC.
III)

264 Estar escaso de dinero
To be just about out of money

265 Estar fuera de la casa
To be out of the house,
away from home

266 Estar fuera de la ley
To be violating the law

267 Estar harto de
To be fed up with

*268 Estar hasta los topes
To be filled up

**269 Estar hecho un costal de
huesos**
To be very thin, nothing but
skin and bones

*270 Estar hecho una sopa
To be sopping wet, soaked
through

271 Estar mal templado
To be in a bad humor

272 Estar muy metido en
To be deeply involved in

273 Estar para
To be about to

274 Estar peor que antes
To be worse off

275 Estar por
To be in favor of

276 Estar ras con ras
To be flush, perfectly even

277 Estar regular
To feel O.K.

278 Estar salado
To be unlucky

279 Estar sobre sí
To be on the alert, cautious

280 Estar torcido con
To be on unfriendly terms
with

281 Estar uno en sus cabales
To be in one's right mind

282 Estar uno hasta el copete
To be stuffed, fed up

283 Estar uno hasta la coronilla
To be fed up, satisfied

284 **Estarse parado**
To stand still

285 **Estirar la pata**
To die

286 **Estola de visón**
A mink wrap

287 **Estrechar la mano (a)**
To shake hands, grasp (or squeeze) a hand

288 **Estrella de mar**
Starfish

289 **Exceso de equipaje**
Excess baggage

290 **Éxito de venta**
Best seller

291 **Explicar una cátedra**
To teach a course

292 **Extranjero de nacimiento**
Foreign born

F

1 **Facilitar todos los datos**
To furnish all the data

2 **Falta de conocimientos**
Lack of instructions

3 **Falta de saber**
Lack of instructions

4 **Faltar a su palabra**
To break one's word

5 **Faltar poco**
It's almost time

6 **Faltarle a uno un tornillo**
To have little sense, "to have a screw loose"

7 **Farol de cola**
Tail light

8 **Farol trasero**
Tail light

9 **Fijarse en**
To notice, pay attention to

10 **Formar parte de**
To be a part (or member) of

11 **Forzar la entrada**
To break into

12 **Franquear el paso**
To permit passage of

13 **Frente a**
In front of

14 **Fruncir el ceño**
To frown, scowl

15 **Fruncir el entrecejo**
To wrinkle one's brow

16 **Fruncir las cejas**
To frown, knit the eyebrows

17 **Fuegos artificiales**
Fireworks

18 **Fuera de broma**
All joking aside

19 **Fuera de lo corriente**
Unusual, out of the ordinary

20 **Fuera de propósito**
Irrelevant

21 **Fuera de sí**
Beside oneself

22 **Fuerza motriz**
Driving force, power

23 **Funda de almohada**
Pillow case

G

1 **(Las) gafas de sol**
Sunglasses

2 **Galas de novia**
Trousseau

3 **Ganar para comer**
To earn a living

4 **Ganar peso**
To put on weight

5 **Ganar tiempo**
To save time

6 **Ganarse la vida**
To make one's living

7 **Gato montés**
Wildcat

8 **Género humano**
Human race

9 **Gente de baja estofa**
Low-class people, rabble

10 **Giro postal**
Postal money order

11 **Gradería cubierta**
Grandstand

12 **Granada de mano**
Hand grenade

13 **Gremio obrero** (or **Gremio de obreros**)
Trade union

14 **Guardar cama**
To stay in bed, to be confined in bed

15 **Guardar silencio**
To keep silent

16 **Guía telefónica**
Telephone book (directory)

17 **Gusano de la conciencia**
Remorse

H

1 **Ha de ser verdad.**
It must be true.

2 **Ha pasado.**
It is all over.

3 **Ha terminado.**
It is all over.

4 **Había una vez** (or: **Érase que se era; Érase una vez; Y va de cuento**)
Once upon a time

5 **Hablar al caso**
To speak to the point, or in plain language

6 **Hablar alto** (or **en voz alta**)
To speak loudly

7 **Hablar en secreto**
To whisper

8 **Hablar para sus adentros**
To talk to oneself

*9 **Hablar por los codos**
To talk too much, chatter constantly

10 **Hace aire.**
It is windy.

11 **Hace (dos, tres, etc.) años**
(Two, three, etc.) years ago

12 **Hace buen (mal) tiempo.**
It is good (bad) weather.

13 **Hace calor.**
It is hot.

14 **Hace caso omiso**
It (he, etc.) ignores

15 **Hace fresco.**
It is cool.

16 **Hace frío.**
It is cold.

17 **Hace mucho que no juego (leo, etc.).**
It is a long time since I played (read, etc.).

18 **Hace mucho tiempo**
Long ago

19 **Hace sol.**
It is sunshiny.

20 **Hace viento.**
It is windy.

21 **Hacer alto**
To stop

22 **Hacer arreglos**
To make arrangements

23 **Hacer buen papel**
To make a good showing

24 **Hacer caso a** (or **Hacer caso de**)
To take into account, pay attention to

25 **Hacer caso omiso de**
To ignore

26 **Hacer cocos**
To make eyes at, flirt

*27 **Hacer cola**
To queue up, form a line

28 **Hacer como si**
To act as if

29 **Hacer cuco a**
To fool, make fun of

30 **Hacer chacota de**
To make fun of

31 **Hacer de**
To act as

32 **Hacer de nuevo**
To do again, to do over

33 **Hacer deducciones precipitadas**
To jump at conclusions

34 **Hacer destacar**
To emphasize

35 **Hacer ejercicio**
To take exercise

36 **Hacer el favor de** (+ inf.)
Please

*37 **Hacer el** (or **Hacer un**) **papel**
To play a role

38 **Hacer el ridículo**
To be ridiculous, act a fool

39 **Hacer escala (en)**
To stop over at, call at a port

40 **Hacer falta**
To lack, be in need of

41 **Hacer favoritismos en prejuicio de**
To discriminate against

42 **Hacer frente (a)**
To face

43 **Hacer gala de**
To boast of

44 **Hacer garras**
To tear to pieces

45 **Hacer gestos**
To make faces at

46 **Hacer gracia**
To amuse, to make laugh

47 **Hacer juego**
To match

48 **Hacer la corte**
To court, woo

49 **Hacer la zanguanga**
To feign illness

*50 **Hacer las maletas**
To pack, get ready to leave

51 **Hacer las paces**
To make up after a quarrel

52 **Hacerlo posible**
To do one's best

53 **Hacer mal papel**
To make a poor showing

54 **Hacer mala obra**
To hinder, interfere

55 **Hacer mella**
To make a dent or impression, to cause pain or worry

56 **Hacer memoria**
To remember, recollect

57 **Hacer muecas**
To make faces

58 **Hacer otra vez**
To do over

59 **Hacer pedazos**
To break into pieces

*60 **Hacer pinta**
To play hooky, cut class

61 **Hacer por escrito**
To put in writing

62 **Hacer preguntas** (or **Hacer una pregunta**)
To ask questions, (to ask a question)

63 **Hacer presa**
To seize

64 **Hacer pretender**
To pretend, feign

*65 **Hacer puente**
To take a long weekend

66 **Hacer rajas**
To slice, to tear or cut into strips

67 **Hacer rostro**
To face

68 **Hacer rumbo a**
To head (or sail) towards

69 **Hacer sombra**
To shade, cast shadow

*70 **Hacer su agosto**
To make hay while the sun shines

71 **Hacer teatro**
To show off

72 **Hacer trizas**
To tear to pieces, to shred

73 **Hacer un pedido**
To place an order

74 **Hacer un trato**
To make a deal

75 **Hacer un viaje**
To go on a journey

76 **Hacer una mala jugada**
To play a mean trick

77 **Hacer una perrada**
To play a mean trick

78 **Hacer una plancha**
To make a ridiculous blunder

79 **Hacer una visita**
To pay a visit

80 **Hacer vida**
To live together

81 **Hacerle daño a uno**
To hurt or harm someone

82 **Hacerle la primera cura a**
To render first aid

83 **Hacerse a**
To get used to

84 **Hacerse a la derecha**
To pull over to the right

85 **¡Hacerse a un lado!**
Step aside!

86 **Hacerse amigo**
To make friends with

87 **Hacerse cargo**
To take charge, to be responsible for

88 **Hacerse de rogar**
To be coaxed, to let oneself (or want to) be coaxed

89 **Hacerse duro**
To resist stubbornly

90 **Hacerse el desentendido**
To pretend not to notice

91 **Hacerse el sordo**
To pretend not to hear, turn a deaf ear

92 **Hacerse el tonto**
To play dumb, to act the fool

93 **Hacerse entender**
To make oneself understood

94 **Hacerse ilusiones**
To fool oneself

95 **Hacerse la raya**
To part one's hair

96 **Hacerse muerto**
To pretend to be dead

97 Hacerse noche
To grow late, get late in the evening

98 Hacerse tarde
To get late

99 Hacerse un lío
To get tangled up, become confused

100 Hacerse uno rajas
To wear oneself out

101 Hacia adelante
Forward

102 Hacia atrás
Backward

103 Hágame el favor de
Please

104 Hasta aquí (or Hasta ahí)
Up to now, so far

105 Hasta cierto punto
In a way, up to a point

106 ¿Hasta dónde?
How far?

107 Hasta más no poder
To the limit, utmost

108 Hasta el tope
Up to the top

109 Hasta la fecha
Up to date, up to now

110 Hasta la vista.
"So long" (Goodbye).

111 Hasta luego.
"So long" (Goodbye — see you later).

112 Hasta que
Until

113 Hasta que se llene
Until full

*114 Hay gato encerrado.
There is more than meets the eye.

115 Hay lodo.
It is muddy.

116 Hay luna.
It is moonlight.

*117 Hay moros en la costa.
Something is wrong.
The coast is not clear.
Little pitchers have big ears.

118 Hay neblina.
It is foggy or misty.

119 Hay polvo.
It is dusty.

120 Hay que
One must, It is necessary to - -

121 Hay (or Hace) sol.
It is sunny.

122 Hay tempestad.
It is storming.

123 Hay tormenta.
It is storming.

124 Hay viento.
It is windy.

125 He aquí
Behold, Here is - - -

126 Hecho y derecho
Mature, full-fledged, grown up

127 Hierro de desecho
Scrap iron

128 Hilera de perlas
String of pearls

129 Hincarse de rodillas
To kneel down

130 Hojuela (or Papel) de estaño (de aluminio)
Tin foil (aluminum foil)

131 Hoy (en) día
Nowadays

132 Hombre de bien
Honesty, honest man

133 Hombre de estado
Statesman

134 Hombre de negocios
Business man

135 Hombre de pro
Man of worth

136 Hombre de provecho
Worthy or useful man

137 Hombre de pulso
Steady, prudent man

138 Huelga decir
Needless to say

139 Huellas digitales
Fingerprints

140 Huevos duros
Hard-boiled eggs

141 Huevos estrellados
Fried eggs

142 Huevos pasado(s) por agua
Soft-boiled eggs

143 Huevos revueltos
Scrambled eggs

I

1 Ida y vuelta
Round-trip ticket

2 Idas y venidas
Goings and comings

3 Igual que
The same as

4 Impedir el paso
To block the door, to obstruct the way

5 Impetu de ira
Fit of anger

6 Impuesto sobre rentas
Income tax

7 Inaplicable al caso
Irrelevant

8 Incurrir en el odio de
To incur the hatred of

9 Incurrir en un error
To fall into (or commit) an error

10 Ingenio de azúcar
Sugar refinery, sugar plantation

11 Ingresar en
To join (a club, etc.)

12 Ir a caballo
To ride horseback

13 Ir a medias (or Ir a la mitad)
To go halves (50-50)

14 Ir a pie
To walk, to go on foot

15 Ir al centro
To go downtown

16 Ir al grano
To get down to cases, come to the point

17 Ir corriendo
To be running

18 Ir de compras
To go shopping

19 Ir de jarana
To go on a spree

20 Ir de pesca
To go fishing

21 Ir de vacaciones
To go on vacation

22 Ir del brazo
To go arm in arm

23 Ir entendiendo
To begin to understand

24 Ir para atrás
To back up

25 Irse (or Andar) a la deriva
To drift, to be adrift

26 Irse a pique
To founder, to sink

27 Irse abajo
To fall down

J

1 Jardín zoológico
Zoo

2 Juego de palabras
Pun, play on words

3 Juego de té
Tea set

4 Juego limpio
Fair play

5 Juego sucio
Foul play

6 Jugador de manos
Juggler

7 Jugar limpio
To play fair

8 Jugarle una mala partida
To play a bad trick on one

9 Junto a
Near to, or next to

10 Junto con
With, along with

11 Jurado de acusación
Grand jury

L

1 La comidilla de la vecindad
The talk of the town

2 La cosa no cuajó.
The thing did not jell (or work well).

3 La cuestión palpitante
The burning question

*4 La gota que derrama el vaso
The last straw, the straw that broke the camel's back

5 La guerra mundial
World war

6 La mayoría (de)
The majority (of), most of

7 La mayor parte (de)
The majority (of), most of

8 La mera idea de
The very thought of

9 La mera verdad
The real truth

10 La rutina diaria
The daily grind

11 La semana antepasada
Week before last

12 La semana entrante
Next week

13 La semana pasada
Last week

14 La semana que viene
Next week

15 La verdad clara y desnuda
The whole truth

16 Labrado en madera
Carving, woodwork

17 Lado de abajo (or Lado inferior)
Underside

18 Lado flaco
Weak side

19 Lancha salvavidas
Life boat

20 Lápiz para los labios
Lipstick

*21 Largas uñas
A thief

22 ¡Largo de aquí!
Get out of here!

23 Largos años
A long time, many years

24 Las posadas
Nine-day Christmas festivities

25 Lavarse las manos
To wash one's hands

26 **Lecciones particulares**
Private lessons

27 **Lengua de tierra**
Neck (or point) of land

28 **Letra abierta**
Letter of credit

29 **Letra de cambio**
Draft, bill of exchange

30 **Letra mayúscula**
Capital letter

31 **Letra minúscula**
Lower-case letter

32 **Letras de molde**
Print, printed letters

33 **Levantar a pulso**
To lift with the wrist or hand

34 **Levantar el campo**
To break camp

35 **Levantar falso testimonio**
To bear false witness

36 **Levantar la mesa**
To clear the table

37 **Levantar la sesión**
To adjourn a meeting

38 **Levantar un plano**
To survey, to map

39 **Levantarse de malas (**or
Levantarse con las malas,
or **Levantarse con el santo**
de espaldas)
To get up on (or out of) the
wrong side of bed

40 **Libre cambio**
Free trade

41 **Libro de caja**
Cash book

42 **Libro en rústica**
Paperback book

43 **Libro mayor**
Ledger

44 **Liga (de goma)**
Rubber band

45 **Ligero de cascos**
Light-hearted, frivolous

46 **Limitación de partos**
Birth control

*47 **Limpio de polvo y paja**
Net, entirely free, clear profit

48 **Lista de comidas**
Bill of fare, menu

49 **Lo antes posible**
The earliest possible

50 **Lo de menos**
Of little importance, the least of it

51 **Lo expuesto**
What has been said

52 **Lo más pronto posible**
As soon as possible

53 **Lo menos posible**
As little as possible

54 **Lo mismo da.**
It makes no difference.

55 **Lo que**
That which

56 **Lo que hizo**
Which caused

57 **Lo recién llegado**
A new arrival

58 **Lo siento mucho.**
I'm very sorry.

59 **Loco de remate**
Stark mad

60 **Los (Las) demás**
The others, the rest of them

61 **Los que**
Those which, those who,
the ones

62 **Luego que**
As soon as

63 **Luna de miel**
Honeymoon

64 **Luz de mano**
Flashlight[8]

LL

1 **Llamada por cobrar**
Toll call

2 **Llamar al pan pan, y al vino vino**
Call a spade a spade

3 **Llamar por teléfono**
To call on the telephone

4 **Llanta de repuesto**
Spare tire

5 **Llave de tuercas**
Wrench

6 **Llave inglesa**
Monkey wrench

7 **Llave maestra**
Master key

8 **Llegar a saber**
To come to know

9 **Llegar a ser**
To become, to get to be

10 **Llenar un vacío**
To bridge a gap

11 **Lleno de bote en bote**
Full to the brim

12 **Llevar a cabo**
To carry through, to accomplish

13 **Llevar a efecto**
To carry out

14 **Llevar cuentas**
To keep accounts

15 **Llevar el compás**
To beat time

16 **Llevar la contra**
To oppose, to object to

17 **Llevar la cuenta (or Llevar cuenta de)**
To keep track of

18 **Llevar puesto**
To wear

19 **Llevar ventaja**
To have the lead, to be ahead

20 **Llevarse adelante**
To carry out

21 **Llevarse bien (con)**
To get along well with

22 **Llevarse un chasco**
To be disappointed, surprised, fooled

*23 **Llover a cántaros**
To rain cats and dogs (pitchforks)

M

1 **Macho y hembra**
Hook and eye

2 **Mal genio**
Bad temper

3 **Mal mandado (or Muy mandado)**
Ill-behaved

4 **Mal ojo**
Evil eye

5 **Mal sufrido**
Impatient

6 **Malas tretas**
Bad tricks, bad habits

7 **Mandar una bofetada**
To slap

8 **Mandar una pedrada**
To throw a stone

9 **Mañana Dios dirá.**
Tomorrow is another day.
Worry tomorrow.

---

[8] or **la lámpara**

10 **Mañana por la mañana (temprano)**
Tomorrow morning (early)

11 **Mañana por la noche**
Tomorrow night

12 **Mañana por la tarde**
Tomorrow afternoon

13 **Máquina de escribir**
Typewriter

14 **Máquina eléctrica de afeitar**
Electric razor

15 **Mar adentro**
Out at sea

16 **Mar de fondo**
Swell of the sea

17 **Marca de fábrica**
Trademark

18 **Marido y mujer**
Man and wife

19 **Marina de guerra**
Navy

20 **Más acá**
Closer

21 **Más acá de**
This side of, before you get to

22 **Más adelante**
Farther on, later on

23 **Más ahorita**
Right now

24 **Más allá (de)**
Beyond, farther away

25 **Más aún**
Furthermore, what is more

26 **Más bien**
Rather

27 **Más bien que**
Rather than

28 **Más de**
More than

29 **Más de una vez**
More than once

30 **Más pesado que una mosca**
Pesky as a fly

31 **Más que**
More than

32 **Más que nadie**
More than anyone

33 **Más que nunca**
More than ever

34 **Más vale**
It is better

35 **Más vale tarde que nunca**
Better late than never

36 **Matar dos pájaros de un tiro**
To kill two birds with one stone

37 **Matar el gusano**
To satisfy a need or desire (hunger, etc.)

38 **Materia prima**
Basic material

39 **Mayor de edad**
Of age, adult

40 **Me alegro mucho de verlo(a).**
I'm very glad to see you.

41 **Me da asco.**
I loathe it. It makes me sick.
It disgusts (nauseates) me.

42 **Me da pena.**
It grieves me.

43 **Me desagrada.**
I don't like it.

44 **Me doy.**
I give up.

45 **Me entró miedo.**
I became afraid.

46 **Me hace falta.**
I need it.

47 **Me lloran los ojos.**
My eyes water.

48 **Me parece que**
It seems to me that

49 **Me repugna.**
I don't like it.

50 **Mecanismo de dirección**
Steering gear

*51 **Media cuchara**
A mediocre person

52 **Medida para áridos**
Dry measure

53 **Medio sordo**
Hard of hearing

54 **Medir las calles**
To walk the streets, be out
of a job

55 **Mejor dicho**
Better yet, rather

*56 **Memoria de gallo**
Poor memory

57 **Menor de edad**
A minor person

58 **Menos de (or Menos que)**
Less than

59 **Menos mal**
At least

60 **Merecer la pena**
To be worthwhile

61 **Meter la pata**
To put one's foot in one's mouth

62 **Meterse con**
To pick a quarrel or fight with

63 **Meterse de por medio**
To intervene, meddle in a
dispute

64 **Meterse en un lío**
To get oneself in a mess

65 **Mi propio carro (casa, etc.)**
My own car (my own house, etc.)

66 **Mientras más - - -
menos**
The more - - - the less - - -

67 **Mientras tanto**
Meanwhile

68 **Mil gracias.**
A thousand thanks.

69 **Ministerio de Relaciones
Exteriores**
Foreign office

70 **Mirada de soslayo**
Side glance

71 **Mirar con el rabo del ojo**
To look out the corner of one's eye

72 **Mirar por alguien**
To take care of someone

73 **Molestarse en**
To bother about

74 **Molino de viento**
Windmill

75 **Moneda corriente**
Currency

76 **Moneda falsa**
Counterfeit

77 **Moneda menuda**
Change, small coins

78 **Moneda suelta**
Change, small coins

79 **Montaña de hielo**
Iceberg

*80 **Montaña rusa**
Roller coaster

81 **Montar en pelo**
To ride bareback

82 **Motejar de**
To brand as

83 **Motor de reacción**
Jet engine

84 **Muchas felicidades.**
Many happy returns.

85 **Muchas gracias.**
Many thanks.

86 **Muchas subidas y bajadas**
Many ups and downs, much
going up and down

87 **Mudar de casa**
To move (change residence)

88 **Muelle real**
Mainspring of a watch

89 **Municiones de guerra**
War supplies

90 **Música del pueblo**
Folk music

91 **Música tradicional**
Folk music

92 **Muy a menudo**
Very often

93 **Muy de mañana**
Very early in the morning

94 **Muy trabajador**
Hard-working

N

*1 **Nacer de pie (or pies)**
To be born lucky

2 **Nada de eso**
Nothing like that

3 **Nada de particular**
Nothing unusual

4 **Nada en absoluto**
Nothing at all

5 **Nada más**
Just, only

6 **Naturaleza muerta**
Still life (re paintings)

*7 **Navaja de afeitar**
Razor

8 **Nave cósmica**
Space ship

9 **Nave cósmica pilotada**
Manned space ship

10 **Navío de guerra**
Warship

11 **Negarse a (contestar)**
To refuse to (answer)

12 **Ni con mucho**
Not by far, not by a long shot

13 **Ni esto ni aquello**
Neither this nor that

14 **Ni mucho menos**
Not by any means, not
anything like it

15 **Ni siquiera**
Not even, even though

16 **Ni yo tampoco.**
Nor I either.

17 **Ningún otro**
Nobody else

18 **No cabe duda (que)**
There is no doubt (that)

19 **No caer bien**
To displease, (with direct
object) not to fit well

20 **No da abasto a**
To be unable to cope with

*21 **No dar pie con bola**
To make a mistake, not to
get things right

22 **No darse cuenta**
Not to realize

23 **No despegar los labios**
Not to say a word, not to
open one's mouth

24 **¡No diga!**
Is that so? You don't say!

25 **No es asunto mío (suyo, etc.).**
It's none of my (your, etc.) business.

26 **No es de mi incumbencia.**
It does not concern me.

27 **No es mucho que**
It is no wonder that

28 **No estar de humor**
To be out of sorts, not in a
laughing mood

29 No estoy de acuerdo.
I disagree.

30 ¡No faltaba más!
That's the last straw! Why the
very idea!

*31 No hallar vado
To find no way out

32 No hay de que.
You're welcome.
Don't mention it.

33 No hay más remedio que
There's no other way but to - - -
There's nothing to do except - - -

34 No hay para que
There's no need to

35 No hay prisa.
There's no hurry.

36 No hay que darle vueltas.
There's no way around it.
There are no two ways about
it.

37 No hay que ser.
Don't be like that.

38 No hay remedio.
It can't be helped.

*39 No hay tu tía.
There is no hope, no way out
of it.

40 ¡No importa!
Never mind!

41 No irle ni venirle a uno
To make no difference to one

42 No le hace.
It doesn't matter.
It makes no difference.

43 No más que
Only[9]

44 No le haga caso.
Pay no attention to him.

45 No me da la gana.
I don't want to.

46 No nos debemos nada.
We are even (quits).

47 No obstante
Notwithstanding,
nevertheless

48 No pararse en pelillos
Not to bother about trifles

49 No poder con
Not to be able to stand,
endure, control, carry

50 No poder con la carga
Not to be able to lift the load,
not equal to the burden

51 No poder más
To be exhausted, "all in"

52 No poder menos de (+ inf.).
Not to be able to help - - -
Ex.: **No puede menos de
hacerlo.**
He can't help doing it.

53 No que yo sepa
Not to my knowledge

54 No quedar otro recurso
No way out, no alternative

55 No querer hacerlo
To be unwilling to do it

56 No saber ni papa (de eso)
To know absolutely nothing
(about that)

57 No saber una jota
Not to know anything

58 No se de usted prisa.
Don't hurry.

59 ¡No se ocupe!
Never mind! Don't worry!

60 ¡No se preocupe usted!
Don't worry!

61 No se trata de eso.
That's not the point;
not the question.

---

[9] or **solo, único, solamente**

62 **No sea que**
Or else, because

63 **No ser cosa de juego**
Not to be a laughing matter

*64 **No ser ni chicha ni limonada**
To be worthless, neither fish nor fowl

65 **No servir para nada**
To be good for nothing

66 **No solo - - - sino también**
Not only - - - but also

67 **No tan a menudo**
Not so often

68 **No tener alternativa (or elección)**
To have no alternative, no way out

69 **No tener entrañas**
To be cruel

70 **No tener nada que ver con**
To have nothing to do with

*71 **No tener pelillos en la lengua**
To speak frankly

72 **No tener razón**
To be wrong

73 **No tener remedio**
To be beyond help or repair

74 **No tener sal en la mollera**
To be dull, stupid

75 **No tenga usted cuidado.**
Don't worry about it.
Forget it.

76 **No tengo (ni) la menor idea.**
I don't have the least idea.

77 **No tiene importancia.**
It's not important.
It doesn't matter.

*78 **No tiene pérdida.**
You can't miss it.

79 **No tiene remedio.**
It can't be helped.
It is hopeless.

*80 **No tiene vuelta de hoja.**
There's no two ways about it.

81 **No vale la pena.**
It's not worthwhile.

82 **No vale un pito**
Not worth a straw

83 **No vale una cuartilla**
Not worth a penny

84 **No ver la hora de**
To be anxious to

85 **No viene al cuento (or No viene al caso).**
It is not opportune, or to the point.

86 **Nombre de bautismo**
Given name

87 **Nombre de pila**
Given name

88 **Novela por entregas**
A serial novel

89 **Nudo ciego**
Hard knot

90 **Nudo corredizo**
Slip knot

91 **Nuevo flamante**
Brand new[10]

92 **Nuez moscada (or Nuez de especial)**
Nutmeg

93 **Número impar (or Número non)**
Odd number, uneven number

O

1 **O sea que**
That is to say

2 **O si no - - -**
Or else

---

[10] or **nuevecito**

3 **Obra maestra**
Masterpiece

4 **Observante de la ley**
Law-abiding

5 **Oficiar de**
To serve as

6 **Oficina de turismo**
Travel bureau

7 **Oír decir que**
To hear that

8 **Oír hablar de**
To hear about

9 **Ojo de agua**
Spring of water

*10 **Ojo de buey**
Porthole

11 **Oler a**
To smell like

12 **Ondulado permanente**
Permanent wave

13 **Optar por**
To choose, decide upon

14 **Ornato de mal gusto**
Gingerbread (excessive
ornamentation)

15 **Oso blanco**
Polar bear

16 **Oso hormiguero**
Anteater

17 **Oso marino**
Seal

18 **Oso pardo**
Grizzly bear

19 **Oso peludo**
Teddy bear

20 **¡Otra, otra!**
Encore!

21 **Otra vez**
Again

---

[11] or **el colibrí, el chuparrosa,
el chupaflor**

P

1 **Padre putativo**
Foster father

2 **Pagadero a la vista**
Payable at sight

3 **Pagado de sí mismo**
To be pleased with oneself

4 **Pagar a plazos**
To pay in installments

5 **Pagar al contado**
To pay by cash

6 **Pagar el pato**
To be the goat, get the blame

7 **Pagar en abonos**
To pay in installments

8 **Pagar los gastos**
To foot the bill,
pay the expenses

9 **Pagar por plazos** (or **Pagar
a plazos**)
To pay in installments

10 **Pagarse de**
To be proud of, or boast of

11 **Pájaro cantor**
Song bird

12 **Pájaro carpintero**
Woodpecker

13 **Pájaro mosca**
Hummingbird[11]

14 **¡Palabrita de honor!**
Word of honor, honestly,
No kidding?

15 **Palanca de cambios**
Shift lever

16 **Palillo de dientes**
Toothpick[12]

17 **Pan de jengibre**
Gingerbread (food)

---

[12] or **el mondadientes**

50

18 **Panza mojada** (or **Espalda mojada**
Wetback[13]

19 **Paños menores**
Underclothes

20 **Papel de cartas**
Stationery

21 **Papel de desecho**
Waste paper, scraps of paper

22 **Papel de estaño**
Tin foil

23 **Papel de estraza**
Brown paper

24 **Papel de fumar** (or **de cigarro**)
Cigarette paper

25 **Papel de lija**
Sandpaper

26 **Papel (de) moneda**
Paper money

27 **Papel (de) secante**
Blotting paper

28 **Papel de seda**
Tissue paper

29 **Papel encerado**
Wax paper

30 **Papel para excusado** (or **Papel sanitario**)
Toilet paper

31 **Papel** (or **Hoja**) **volante**
Handbill, circular

32 **Para mis adentros**
To myself

33 **Para que**
In order that

34 **¿Para qué?**
What for?, For what use?

35 **¿Para qué lo usan?**
What is it used for?

36 **¿Para qué se usa?**
What is it used for?

37 **¿Para qué sirve?**
What is it good for?

38 **Para** (or **Por**) **siempre** (+ **jamás**)
Forever (forever and ever)

39 **Para todos lados**
To right and left, on all sides

40 **Para unos fines u otros**
For one purpose or another

41 **Para variar**
For a change

*42 **Parar en seco**
To stop short or suddenly

43 **Parar mientes en**
To consider, reflect on

44 **Pararse en pelillos**
To split hairs

*45 **Parece mentira**
It seems to be impossible

46 **Parecido a**
Like, similar to

47 **Pared medianera**
Partition wall

48 **Partida** (or **Certificado**) **de defunción**
Death certificate

49 **Partida doble**
Double-entry bookkeeping

50 **Pasado de moda**
Out of style, out of date

51 **Pasado mañana**
Day after tomorrow

52 **Pasar a mejor vida**
To die

53 **Pasar como un relámpago**
To flash by

54 **Pasar de la raya**
To overstep bounds, take undue liberties

---

[13] or **los alambres**

55 **Pasar de moda**
To go out of style

56 **Pasar el rato**
To while away time

57 **Pasar la noche en claro**
(or **en blanco**)
Not to sleep a wink

58 **Pasar lista**
To call the roll

59 **Pasar por alto** (or ¡ - - - !)
To omit, overlook, (Halt!)

60 **Pasar por las armas**
To execute

61 **Pasar revista a**
To review, to go over carefully

62 **Pasar un buen rato**
To have a good time

63 **Pasarse sin**
To do without

64 **Pascua de Navidad**
Christmas

65 **Pase usted**
Come in

66 **Pasear a pie**
To take a walk

67 **Pasear en coche**
To go for a drive (by auto)

68 **Pasearse a caballo**
To go horseback riding

69 **Pasearse en automóvil**
To take auto ride

*70 **Paso a nivel**
Grade crossing

71 **Pata de gallo**
Crow's foot wrinkles

*72 **Patas arriba**
Upside down

73 **Patín de ruedas**
Roller skates

74 **Patrón de oro**
Gold standard

75 **Pavo real**
Peacock

76 **Pecar de bueno**
To be too good

77 **Pecar de oscuro**
To be very unclear, too
complicated

78 **Pedir prestado**
To borrow

79 **Pegar de soslayo**
To glance, to hit at a slant

80 **Pegar fuego**
To set afire

81 **Pegar un chasco**
To play a trick, surprise,
disappoint

82 **Pegar un salto**
To take a jump

83 **Pegar un susto**
To give a scare

84 **Pena capital**
Capital punishment

85 **Pena de muerte**
Capital punishment

86 **Pensar en**
To intend, to think about

87 **Pensión completa**
Room and board

88 **Peor que**
Worse than

89 **Peor que peor**
That is even worse.

90 **Perder cuidado**
Not to worry

91 **Perder de vista**
To lose sight of

92 **Perder el juicio**
To lose one's mind, go crazy

93 **Perder el tiempo**
To lose time

94 **Perder el tren**
To miss the train

95 **Perder la razón**
To lose one's mind

96 **Perder la vista**
To go blind

97 **Perder prestigio**
To lose face

98 **Perderse de vista**
To vanish, to be lost from
view, to drop out of sight

99 **Perro mestizo**
Mongrel dog

100 **Pesarle a uno**
To be sorry for someone, to
regret

101 **Peso bruto**
Gross weight

102 **Pestillo de golpe**
Spring latch

103 **Petróleo crudo**
Crude oil

*104 **Piano de cola**
Grand piano

105 **Piano de media cola**
Baby grand piano

106 **Piano vertical**
Upright piano

107 **Picar en**
To border on

108 **Picar muy alto**
To aim very high

109 **Piedra angular** (or **Piedra
fundamental**)
Cornerstone

110 **Piedra caliza**
Limestone

111 **Piedra pómez**
Pumice

112 **(X) Pies de altura** (or de
alto)
(X) Feet tall

113 **(X) Pies de largo**
(X) Feet long

*114 **Pillar una mona**
To get drunk

115 **Pintar venado**
To play hooky

*116 **Pintarle un violín**
To break one's word

*117 **Pintor de brocha gorda**
House painter, or poor artist

118 **Pintura al óleo**
Oil painting

119 **Piso bajo**
Ground floor

120 **Piso principal**
Main floor (usually second
floor)

121 **Pista de aterrizaje**
Landing strip

122 **Placa de circulación**
License plate

123 **Plan de estudios** (or
Programa de estudios)
Course of study, curriculum

124 **Plancha de blindaje**
Armor plate

*125 **Planchar el asiento**
To be a wallflower

126 **Planta baja**
Ground floor

127 **Plata de ley**
Sterling silver

128 **Plataforma de lanzamiento**
Launching pad

129 **Plaza de toros**
Bullring

130 **Pleito de acreedores**
Bankruptcy proceedings

131 **Poca cosa**
Not much

132 **Poco a poco**
Gradually, little by little

133 **Poco después (de)**
Shortly thereafter

134 **Poco para las (tres)**
To be nearly (3) o'clock

135 **Poco rato**
Very soon

136 **Póliza de seguros**
Insurance policy

137 **Polvos para dientes**
Tooth powder

138 **Poner a buen recaudo**
To place in safety

139 **Poner adelantado**
To set forward (e.g., a clock)

140 **Poner al corriente**
To inform, to bring up to date

141 **Poner al punto un motor**
To tune up a motor

142 **Poner al tablero**
To risk, endanger

143 **Poner casa**
To set up housekeeping

*144 **Poner cuernos a**
To be unfaithful (to a
husband), to deceive

145 **Poner defectos (or Poner
faltas)**
To find fault with

146 **Poner el grito en el cielo**
To complain loudly, to "hit
the ceiling"

147 **Poner en claro**
To clear up, to clarify

148 **Poner en conocimiento**
To inform

149 **Poner en duda**
To question, to doubt

150 **Poner en el cielo**
To praise, extol

151 **Poner en infusión**
To steep (tea leaves)

152 **Poner en juego**
To set in motion, to
coordinate

153 **Poner en limpio**
To make a clean copy,
to re-copy

154 **Poner en marcha**
To get going

155 **Poner en razón**
To pacify

156 **Poner en ridículo**
To humiliate, make a fool of

157 **Poner faltas**
To find fault with

158 **Poner (imp. "Pon") la luz,
(el radio, T.V., etc.)**
To turn on the light, (radio,
T.V., etc.)

159 **Poner la mesa**
To set the table

160 **Poner la mira**
To fix one's eyes on, aim at

161 **Poner más alto (bajo) el
radio**
To turn up (down) radio, etc.

*162 **Poner pies en polvorosa**
To take to one's heels

163 **Poner pleito**
To bring charges or a lawsuit
against

164 **Poner por las nubes**
To praise to the skies

165 **Poner por obra**
To undertake, put into
practice

166 **Poner todo de su parte**
To do one's best

167 Poner una queja
To file a complaint

168 Ponerse a
To begin, start

169 Ponerse bien
To get well

170 Ponerse colorado
To blush

171 Ponerse chango
To be alert, wary

172 Ponerse de acuerdo
To come to an agreement

173 Ponerse de pie
To get to one's feet

174 Ponerse de rodillas
To kneel

175 Ponerse duro
To resist stubbornly

176 Ponerse en
To reach

177 Ponerse en camino
To set out (on a trip, etc.)

178 Ponerse en contra de
To oppose, be against

179 Ponerse en marcha
To start, start out

180 Ponerse en pie
To get up, or rise

181 Por acá (or Por aquí)
This way, over here

182 Por accidente (or Por casualidad)
By accident

183 Por adelantado
In advance

184 Por ahí (or Por allá)
Over there, about that

185 Por ahora
For the time being, for now

186 Por algo
For some reason, That's why

187 Por allí
That way

188 Por aquí
This way

189 Por aquí cerca
Around here, in this vicinity

190 Por arriba
Above

191 Por asuntos ajenos a mi voluntad
Because of things or events beyond my control

192 Por carga
By freight

193 Por casualidad
By chance, by accident

194 Por ciento
Per cent

195 Por completo
Completely

196 Por conducto de
Through

197 Por (or En) consecuencia de
Therefore, consequently

198 Por consiguiente
Consequently, therefore

199 Por de (or Por lo) pronto
For the present

200 Por delante
Ahead

201 Por dentro
On the inside

202 Por desgracia
Unfortunately

203 Por despecho
Out of spite

204 Por detrás
From the rear

205 Por día
By the day

206 **¿Por dónde?**
Where, through, which?
Which way?

207 **Por duplicado**
In duplicate

208 **Por ejemplo**
For example

209 **Por el contrario**
On the contrary

210 **Por el momento**
For the time being

211 **Por el estilo**
Such as that, of that kind

212 **Por el (or Por la, or Por lo) presente**
For the present

213 **Por encima de**
On top of

214 **Por encima de todo**
Above all

215 **Por ende**
Hence, therefore

216 **Por entre**
Among, between

217 **Por esa razón**
For that reason, that is why

218 **Por escrito**
In writing

219 **Por eso**
For that reason, therefore

220 **Por extenso**
In detail, at length

221 **Por favor**
Please

222 **Por ferrocarril**
By rail

223 **Por fin**
At last, finally

224 **Por fuera**
From the outside, on the outside

225 **Por hoy**
At present

226 **Por instantes**
Continually, moment to moment

227 **Por la mañana (or Por la tarde, etc.)**
In the morning, (afternoon, etc.)

228 **Por la mitad**
In half, in the middle

229 **Por la noche (or En la noche)**
At night, in the evening

230 **Por las buenas o por las malas**
Whether one likes it or not

231 **Por las nubes**
Sky-high

232 **Por lo común**
Generally

233 **Por lo cual**
Therefore

234 **Por lo demás**
Moreover, as for the rest (of us), aside from this

235 **Por lo general**
Usually, generally

236 **(Al) por mayor**
At (or by) wholesale

237 **(Al) por menor**
At (or by) retail

238 **Por lo menos**
At least

239 **Por lo pronto**
For the time being

240 **Por lo regular**
Usually, as a rule

241 **Por lo que**
Because of which

242 **Por lo que pueda tronar**
Just in case

243 Por lo tanto
Therefore

244 Por lo visto
Apparently, by the looks of, evidently

245 Por más que
However much

246 Por medio de
By means of

247 Por menudo
In detail, retail

248 Por mí mismo(a)
By myself

249 Por mi parte
As far as I'm concerned

250 Por motivo
On account of

251 Por mucho que
No matter how much

252 Por ningún lado
Nowhere

253 Por ningún motivo
Under no circumstances, no matter what

254 Por otra parte
On the other hand

255 Por otro lado
On the other hand (or side)

256 Por poco
Almost, nearly[14]
Ex.: **Por poco se muere.**
He almost died.

257 Por primera vez
For the first time

258 ¿Por qué?
Why?

259 Por rareza
Seldom

260 Por regla general
As a general rule, usually

---
[14] or **casi**

261 Por separado
Separately

262 Por si acaso
In case, just in case

263 Por sí mismo(a)
By oneself

264 Por su cuenta
All by himself (oneself)

265 Por su mano
By oneself

266 Por supuesto
Of course

267 Por término medio
On an average

268 Por (or A or En) todas partes
All over, everywhere

269 Por toda suerte de penalidades
Through thick and thin

270 Por todo el mundo
All over the world

271 Por todo lo alto
Not sparing expense

272 Por todos lados
All over, everywhere, all sides

273 Por última vez
For the last time, finally

274 Por último
Finally, at last

275 Por ventura
Perchance

276 Porción de gente
A lot of people

277 Porque si no
Otherwise

278 Práctico de puerto
Harbor pilot

279 Prefiero que no - - -
I would rather not

280 Preguntar por
To ask about

281 **Prender el fuego**
To start the fire

282 **Prender fuego a**
To set fire to

283 **Preocuparse de**
To take care of

284 **Preocuparse por**
To worry about, to be
concerned about or for

285 **Presencia de ánimo**
Presence of mind, serenity

286 **Prestar atención**
To pay attention

287 **Primer término**
Foreground

288 **Primera velocidad**
Low gear

289 **Primeros auxilios**
First aid

290 **Prisión perpetua**
Life imprisonment

291 **Proceso verbal**
Minutes, record

292 **Profundamente dormido**
Fast asleep

293 **Prohibida la entrada**
No trespassing

294 **Prohibido el paso**
No trespassing, Keep out

295 **Prohibido estacionarse**
No parking

296 **Propulsión a chorro**
Jet propulsion

297 **Propulsión a cohete**
Rocket propulsion

298 **Proyecto de ley**
Bill (legislature)

299 **Puede ser que**
It may be that

300 **¿Puedo servirle en algo?**
May I help you?

301 **Puente colgante**
Suspension bridge

302 **Puente levadizo**
Drawbridge

303 **Puerco espín**
Porcupine

304 **Puerta accesoria** (or **Puerta falsa**)
Side door

305 **Puerta franca**
Open door, free entry

306 **Puerta trasera**
Back door

307 **Puerto franco**
Free port

308 **Pues bien**
Now then, well then, all right then

309 **Pues mire**
Well - - - look

310 **Pues que(?)**
Since, so what?

311 **Puesta del sol**
Sunset

312 **Puesto de periódicos**
Newsstand

313 **Puesto de socorro**
First-aid station

314 **Puesto que**
Although, since

315 **Punto de inspección**
Checkpoint

Q

1 **Que** (+ subj. v.)
Let him (or them, etc.) do
something; or May he (they,
you, etc.) be or do something
Ex.: **¡Que se divierta!**
May you have a good time!

2 **¡Qué barbaridad!**
What nonsense! What an
atrocity!

3 **¡Qué batingue!**
What a mess!

4 **¡Qué de!**
What a lot! How much!

5 **¡Qué desgracia!**
How unfortunate!

6 **¡Qué divinidad!**
What a beauty!

7 **¡Qué gorrito!**
That's enough. Stop it.
Cut it out!

8 **¡Qué gusto!**
What a pleasure. I am delighted!

9 **¿Qué haces?**
What's the matter? What is it?

10 **¿Qué hay?**
What's the matter?

11 **¿Qué hay de malo con eso?**
What's wrong with that? So,
what's so bad about that?

12 **¿Qué hay de nuevo?**
What's new(s)?

13 **¿Qué hora es? (or ¿Qué horas son?)**
What time is it?

14 **¡Qué horror!**
How awful!

15 **¿Qué hubo?**
How goes it? What's up?

16 **¡Qué lástima!**
Too bad! What a pity!

17 **¿Qué le debo?**
How much do I owe you?

18 **¿Qué le parece?**
What do you think of it?
How do you like - - -?

19 **¿Qué le pasa (a Ud.)?**
What's the matter with you?

20 **Que le vaya bien**
Good luck

21 **Que lo pase bien.**
Have a good day, etc.

22 **Que llueva o no**
Rain or shine

23 **¡Qué más da!**
What's the difference?

*24 **¿Qué mosca te ha picado?**
What's eating you?

25 **¡Qué nombrecito!**
What a tongue-twister!
(cf. SEC. III)

26 **¿Qué pasa?**
What's up? What's going on?

27 **¿Qué pasó?**
What happened?

28 **¿Qué quiere decir?**
What does it mean?

29 **¿Qué quiere Ud. decir?**
What do you mean?

30 **¿Qué se le ofrece?**
What can I do for you? What can I
show you? What can I serve you?
What would you like to buy?

31 **¿Qué sé yo?**
How should I know?

32 **¿Qué significa?**
What does it mean?

33 **¿Qué tal?**
Hello! How are you?

34 **¿Qué tiene de malo?**
What's wrong with - - -?

35 **¿Qué vale ésto?**
How much is this?

36 **¿Qué ventaja (or objecto) tiene?**
What is the use of it?

37 **Quebrarse uno la cabeza**
To rack one's brain

38 **Quedar bien (con)**
To come out well, (to get along well with)

39 **Quedar contento con**
To be pleased with

40 **Quedar en**
To agree (to)

41 **Quedar entendido que**
To be understood, agreed to

42 **Quedarle bien**
To be becoming

43 **Quedarse con (re una cosa)**
To keep, to take (e.g., I'll take it.)

44 **Quedarse en la casa**
To stay in

*45 **Quedarse uno chato**
To be left in the lurch, disappointed

46 **Quejarse de**
To complain of

47 **Quemarse hasta el suelo**
To burn down

*48 **Quemarse las pestañas**
To burn midnight oil, study hard

49 **Querer decir**
To mean, signify

50 **¿Quién sabe?**
Who knows? I don't know.

*51 **¿Quién te mete, Juan Copete?**
Mind your own business. What's it to you?

52 **Quieras que no (fam.)**
Whether you wish or not

53 **Quiere llover**
It is trying (is about) to rain

54 **Quince días**
Two weeks

55 **¡Quita allá!**
Don't tell me that!

56 **Quitar la mesa**
To clear the table

57 **Quitarse uno un peso de encima**
To be relieved of, to be a load off one's mind

58 **¡Quitarse de aquí!**
Get out of here!

59 **Quitarse de una cosa**
To give up (or get rid of) something

R

1 **Rabiar por**
To be very eager to (or for)

2 **Rara vez (or Raras veces)**
Seldom[15]

3 **Rayos infrarrojos**
Infrared rays

4 **Raíz cuadrada**
Square root

5 **Ratos perdidos**
Leisure hours

6 **Razón social**
Firm name

7 **Rebaja de (x) centavos**
(x) Cents off

8 **Rebajar la paga**
To dock the wages

9 **Receptor telefónico**
Telephone receiver

10 **Recibir manutención gratuita**
To be on relief

11 **Recibir noticias (de)**
To hear from

12 **Recuerdos a**
Regards to - - -

13 **Rechinar los dientes**
To gnash one's teeth

---

[15] or **raramente**

14 **Recién casados**
Newlyweds

15 **Reconocimiento médico**
Physical examination

16 **Refrendar un pasaporte**
To visé (visa) a passport

17 **Refugio antiaéreo**
Bomb shelter

18 **Regentar una cátedra**
To teach a course

19 **Reírse de**
To laugh at

20 **Reírse para sus adentros**
To laugh up one's sleeve

21 **Reloj de pulsera**
Wristwatch

22 **Reloj de sol**
Sundial

23 **Reloj despertador**
Alarm clock

*24 **Remolino de gente**
Throng, crowd

25 **Reparto de correo**
Mail delivery

26 **Repetidas veces**
Over and over again,
various times

27 **Repetir de carretilla**
To rattle off, repeat
mechanically

28 **Repisa** (or **Antepecho**) **de
ventana**
Windowsill

29 **Repítamelo, por favor**
Please say it again

30 **Requisito previo**
Prerequisite

31 **Resarcirse de**
To make up for

32 **Reservar pasaje**
To book passage

33 **Respecto a**
With regard to, concerning,
about

34 **Reunión de confianza**
Informal gathering or party

35 **Reventar de risa**
To burst with laughter

36 **Río abajo**
Down stream

37 **Río arriba**
Up stream

38 **Rodadura de neumático**
Tire tread

39 **Rodaje de película**
Filming of a movie

40 **Romper a**
To start to

41 **Romper el alba**
To dawn

42 **Romperse los cascos**
To rack one's brain

43 **Ropa blanca**
Linen

44 **Ropa interior**
Underclothing

45 **Rosario de desdichas**
Chain of misfortunes

46 **Rozarse con alguien**
To have connections (or
dealings) with someone

S

1 **Sabe bien**
It tastes good

2 **Saber** (+ <u>inf.</u>)
To know how to

3 **Saber a**
To taste like

4 **Saber de memoria**
To know by heart

5 **Sacar a bailar**
To ask to dance

6 **Sacar a luz**
To publish

7 **Sacar a plaza**
To bring out into the open

8 **Sacar a uno de quicio**
To exasperate someone

9 **Sacar el cuerpo**
To dodge

10 **Sacar en claro** (or **en limpio**)
To deduce, conclude[16]

11 **Sacar punta a un lápiz**
To sharpen a pencil

12 **Sacar una fotografía**
To take a picture

13 **Saco de noche**
Overnight bag, satchel

14 **Sala de espera**
Waiting room

15 **Sala de justicia**
Courtroom

16 **Sala de recibo**
Reception room

17 **Salida de pie de banco**
Silly remark, nonsense

18 **Salida del sol**
Sunrise

19 **Salir a**
To resemble, take after

20 **Salir a gatas**
To crawl out of a difficulty

21 **Salir al encuentro de**
To go out to meet, to oppose,
take stand against

22 **Salir bien**
To be successful, to come
out well

23 **Salir de**
To leave, depart

24 **Salir del paso**
To get out of a difficulty

25 **Salir fiador de**
To vouch for

26 **Salir ganando**
To win, to come out ahead

27 **Salir mal**
To fail, to come out poorly

28 **Salirse con la suya**
To have one's own way

29 **Salón de belleza**
Beauty parlor

30 **Saltar a la vista**
To be obvious

31 **Saltar a tierra**
To disembark, to land

32 **Saltar las trancas**
To lose patience, lose one's head

33 **Salto de agua**
Waterfall

34 **Salvar el pellejo**
To save one's skin

35 **Sanidad pública**
Health department

36 **Sano y salvo**
Safe and sound

37 **Santo y bueno**
Well and good

38 **Se aguó la fiesta**
The party was spoiled

39 **Se alquila**
For rent

40 **Se conoce (que)**
It is obvious

41 **Se dice**
It is said, They say

42 **Se ha acabado.**
It is all over.

---

[16] or **concluir, terminar,** etc.

43 **Se habla español.**
Spanish is spoken.

44 **Se me figura**
I guess, I think, I imagine

45 **Se me hace agua la boca.**
My mouth waters.

46 **Se me pasó decirte (fam.).**
I forgot to tell you.

47 **Se prohibe (fumar)**
It is forbidden, - no - (smoking, etc.)

48 **Se solicita**
Wanted

49 **Se suena que**
It is rumored that

50 **Se ve que**
It is obvious that

51 **Se venció el plazo.**
The time limit expired.

52 **Se vende**
For sale

53 **Seguir las pisadas**
To follow in footsteps, emulate

54 **Según y conforme (or Según y como)**
Exactly as, just as, that depends

55 **Seguro contra incendios**
Fire insurance

56 **Seguro de vida**
Life insurance

57 **Seguro que están**
I bet they are

58 **Seguro que sí**
Of course

59 **Seguro sobre la vida**
Life insurance

60 **Sentar bien a**
To fit well

61 **Sentarle bien**
To be becoming

62 **Sentarse en cuclillas**
To squat

63 **Sentir en el alma**
To be terribly sorry, to regret very much

64 **Sentirse destemplado**
Not to feel well, to feel feverish

65 **Ser aficionado a**
To be a fan, a buff

*66 **Ser como un puño**
To be stingy

67 **Ser conocedor**
To be judge of

68 **Ser de rigor**
To be indispensable, to be required by custom

69 **Ser de (or Ser para) ver**
Worth seeing

70 **Ser duro de mollera**
To be stubborn

71 **Ser fuerza**
To be necessary

72 **Ser gente**
To be cultured, socially important

73 **Ser huésped en su casa**
To be seldom at home

74 **Ser oriundo de**
To hail from, come from

75 **Ser piedra de escándalo**
To be the object of scandal

*76 **Ser plato de segunda mesa**
To play second fiddle

77 **Ser tempranero**
To be an early riser

78 **Ser un bofe**
To be a bore, to be repulsive

*79 **Ser un cero a la izquierda**
To be of no account

*80 **Ser un erizo**
To be irritable, harsh

81 **Ser una mujer hacendosa**
To be a good housekeeper

82 **Servicio de mesa**
Set of dishes

83 **Servidor de usted**
At your service

84 **Servir de**
To serve, act as, be used as

85 **Servir la mesa**
To wait table

86 **Servir para**
To be good for, used for

87 **Si acaso**
If at all

88 **Si alguna vez**
If even

89 **Si bien**
Although

90 **Si mal no recuerdo**
If I remember correctly

91 **Si me hace el favor**
If you would do me the favor

92 **Si no**
Or else

93 **Si no compra no magulle.**
Don't handle the merchandise
(fruit, etc.).

94 **Si no fuera por**
Except for

95 **Si no fuera porque**
Except for

96 **¡Si ya te lo dije! (fam.)**
But I already told you!

97 **Siempre que**
Whenever, provided that,
as long as

98 **Siempre y cuando**
Provided

99 **Signo de interrogación**
Question mark

100 **Silla de montar**
Saddle

101 **Sin ceremonia**
Informal

102 **Sin comentarios**
No comment

103 **Sin contar**
Exclusive of

104 **Sin disputa**
Without question

105 **Sin embargo**
However, nevertheless

106 **Sin falta**
By all means, without fail,
without fault

107 **Sin fin**
An infinite quantity

108 **Sin hacer caso de**
Regardless of

109 **Sin igual**
Unequaled

110 **Sin novedad**
As usual (to be well, in good
health)

111 **Sin par**
Peerless, without equal

112 **Sin que**
Without

113 **Sin qué ni para qué**
Without rhyme or reason

114 **Sin querer**
Unwillingly

*115 **Sin rebozo**
Openly, frankly

116 **Sin recurso**
Without remedy, without
appeal

117 **Sin remedio**
Unavoidable, without help

118 **Sin reserva**
Unreserved, frankly

119 **Sin sentir**
Without realizing, inadvertently, unnoticed

120 **Sin ton ni son**

Without rhyme or reason

121 **Sino que**
But

122 **Sírvase usted.**
Help yourself.

123 **Sírvase usted hacerlo.**
Please do it.

124 **So capa de**
Under the guise of

125 **So color de**
Under the pretext of

126 **So pena de**
Under penalty of

127 **So pretexto de**
Under pretext (or pretense) of

128 **Sobradas veces**
Repeatedly, many times

129 **Sobre manera**
Excessively

130 **Sobre mi palabra**
Upon my honor

131 **Sobre que**
Besides, in addition to

132 **Sobre seguro**
Without risk

133 **Sobre todo**
Especially, above all
(**sobretodo** m. = overcoat)

134 **Sociedad anónima (**abbr.
S.A.)
Stock company

135 **Soldado de línea**
Regular soldier

136 **Soldado raso**
Private soldier

137 **Sólo para personas mayores (**or **Sólo para adultos)**
Adults only

138 **Soltar el hervor**
To come to a boil

139 **Soltar la rienda**
To let loose, act without restraint

140 **Sombrero de copa**
Top hat

141 **Sombrero hongo**
Derby hat

142 **Sonar a**
To sound like, seem like

143 **Soñar con (**or **Soñar en)**
To dream of

144 **Soñar despierto**
To daydream

145 **Su punto flaco**
His weakness, his weak side

146 **Su seguro servidor**
Yours truly

147 **Subidas y bajadas**
Ups and downs

148 **Subir al tren**
To get on the train

149 **Subir de punto**
To increase, get worse

150 **Subirse de tono**
To put on airs

151 **Suceda lo que suceda**
Come what may, no matter what

152 **Sudar la gota gorda**
To sweat profusely, work hard, sweat blood, have a bad time

153 **Suerte negra**
Very bad luck

154 **Suma atención**
Close attention

155 **Supuesto que**
Supposing that, since

156 Surtir efecto
To come out as desired or
expected, to give
good results

157 Surtir un pedido
To fill an order

158 Suspender los pagos
To stop payment

T

1 Tabla (or Mesa) de planchar
Ironing board

**2 Tablilla para anuncios (or
Tablilla para avisos)**
Bulletin board[17]

3 Tablero de mano
Control panel

4 Taco de billar
Billiard (pool) cue

5 Tal como (or Tales como)
Such as

6 Tal cual
Such as, so-so, fair

7 Tal para cual
Two of a kind

8 Tal vez
Maybe, perhaps[18]

9 Tal vez sea que
It may be that

10 Taller mecánico
Mechanic's shop

11 Tamaño disparate
Such a big mistake

12 Tambor de freno
Brake drum

13 Tan pronto como
As soon as

14 Tanto - - - como
As much - - - as

15 Tanto mejor
So much the better

16 Tanto peor
So much the worse

17 Tardar en
To be long in, take a long
time (in doing)

18 Tarde o temprano
Sooner or later

19 Tarjeta de crédito
Credit card

20 Tarjeta postal
Postcard

21 Tela adhesiva
Adhesive tape

22 Tela de cebolla
Onion skin, flimsy fabric

23 Tela metálica
Wire screen

24 Temblor de tierra
Earthquake[19]

25 Témpano de hielo
Block of ice, iceberg

26 Tenedor de libros
Bookkeeper

27 Teneduría de libros
Bookkeeping

28 Tener a la vista
To have in sight, to have
received a letter

29 Tener a raya
To keep in bounds, hold in check

30 Tener al corriente
To keep up-to-date, (informed,
posted)

31 Tener - - - años
To be - - - years old

---

[17] or **el tablero**
[18] or **acaso,** or **quizás**

[19] or **el terremoto**

32 **Tener bascas**
To be nauseated

33 **Tener buen éxito**
To make good, succeed

34 **Tener buena cara**
To look well

35 **Tener cabida con alguien**
To have influence with someone

36 **Tener calor**
To be hot

37 **Tener canilla**
To have physical strength

38 **Tener celos**
To be jealous

39 **Tener confianza con**
To be on intimate terms with

40 **Tener cosquillas**
To be ticklish

41 **Tener cuidado (con)**
To take care, watch out (for)

42 **Tener deseos de**
To want to, to be eager to

*43 **Tener el pico de oro**
To be eloquent

44 **Tener en cuenta**
To consider, to take into account

45 **Tener en la mente**
To have in mind

46 **Tener en la punta de la lengua**
To have on the tip of one's tongue

47 **Tener en mucho**
To esteem highly

48 **Tener en poco a**
To hold in low esteem

49 **Tener entendido que**
To understand that - - -

50 **Tener éxito**
To be successful

51 **Tener frío**
To be cold

52 **Tener gana(s) de**
To feel like

53 **Tener gancho**
To be attractive, alluring

54 **Tener gracia**
To be funny

55 **Tener gusto en**
To be glad to

56 **Tener hambre**
To be hungry

57 **Tener la bondad de (+ inf.)**
To be good enough to

58 **Tener la costumbre de**
To be used to - - -

59 **Tener la culpa**
To be to blame

60 **Tener la intención de**
To intend or mean to

61 **Tener la lengua larga**
To have a big mouth

62 **Tener la pena de**
To have the misfortune to

*63 **Tener la vida en un hilo**
To be in great danger

64 **Tener lástima de**
To feel sorry for, take pity on

65 **Tener lugar**
To take place

66 **Tener mal de garganta**
To have a sore throat

*67 **Tener malas pulgas**
To be ill-tempered

68 **Tener miedo**
To be afraid

69 **Tener mucha pena**
To be very sorry

70 **Tener mucho copete**
To be arrogant, haughty

71 **Tener murria**
To be sulky, to have the blues

72 **Tener por**
To believe, judge, consider,
to take for a - - -

73 **Tener presente (de or que)**
To bear in mind

74 **Tener prisa**
To be in a hurry

75 **Tener probabilidad**
To stand a chance

*76 **Tener puños**
To be strong, courageous

77 **Tener que (+ inf.)**
To have to (do something)

78 **Tener que ver (con)**
To have to do with

79 **Tener razón**
To be right

80 **Tener roce con**
To have contact with a person

81 **Tener sed**
To be thirsty

82 **Tener sueño**
To be sleepy

83 **Tener suerte**
To be lucky

84 **Tener tiempo libre**
To have time off

85 **Tener vergüenza**
To be shy, to be ashamed

86 **Tenerle tirria a una persona**
To have dislike for (or grudge
against) a person

87 **Tenerse en pie**
To keep one's feet

88 **Tengo mucho gusto en
conocerle.**
I'm very pleased to make
your acquaintance.

89 **Terrón de azúcar**
Cube of sugar

90 **Testigo de cargo**
Witness for the prosecution

91 **Testigo de vista**
Eye witness

92 **Testigo ocular**
Eye witness

93 **Tez blanca**
Fair complexion

94 **Tiempo claro (or Tiempo
despejado)**
Fine weather

95 **Tierra adentro**
Inland

96 **Tierra de las hadas**
Fairyland

97 **Tierra firme**
Mainland, solid ground

*98 **Tío vivo**
Merry-go-round

99 **Tipo de cambio**
Rate of exchange (re money)

100 **Tirar de**
To pull

101 **Tirar las riendas**
To restrain, tighten the reins

102 **Tirarse una plancha**
To put oneself in a ridiculous
situation

103 **Tocar de oído**
To play be ear

104 **Tocar en lo vivo**
To hurt to the quick, touch a
very sensitive spot

105 **Tocar por fantasía**
To play by ear

106 **Tocarle a uno**
To be one's turn

107 **Tocarle a uno la suerte**
To be one's turn, to fall to
one's lot, to be lucky

108 **Tocarse el sombrero**
To tip one's hat

109 **Toda clase de**
All kinds of

110 **Todas las veces (que)**
Every time, whenever

111 **Todavía no**
Not yet

112 **Todo el año**
All year round

113 **Todo el día**
All day

114 **Todo el mundo**
Everybody

115 **Todo el que**
Everybody who

116 **Todo el tiempo**
All the time

117 **Todo hombre**
Everyone

118 **Todo lo contrario**
Exactly the opposite

119 **Todo lo demás**
Everything else

120 **Todo lo posible**
All that is possible

121 **Todo sigue bien**
All goes well

122 **Todos los días**
Every day

123 **Toma de corriente**
Electric plug or outlet

124 **Tomar a broma**
To take as a joke

125 **Tomar a pecho(s)**
To take to heart

126 **Tomar a risa**
To laugh off, take lightly

127 **Tomar agua (cerveza, café, etc.)**
To drink water, (beer, coffee, etc.)

128 **Tomar el pelo**
To tease

*129 **Tomar el rábano por las hojas**
To put the cart before the horse, to misinterpret or misconstrue

130 **Tomar el sol**
To sunbathe

131 **Tomar en cuenta**
To consider, take into account

132 **Tomar en serio**
To take to heart

133 **Tomar la delantera**
To take the lead

134 **Tomar por la derecha**
To turn to the right

135 **Tomar por su cuenta**
To attend to personally

136 **Tomar tiempo libre**
To take time off

137 **Tomar tierra**
To land

138 **Tomar un partido**
To decide

139 **Tomar una providencia**
To take a step, to measure

140 **Tomarlo con calma**
To take it easy

141 **Tonto de capirote**
Dunce, plain fool

142 **Tornar a hacerlo**
To do it again

143 **Tos ferina**
Whooping cough

144 **Traer puesto**
To wear, to have on

145 **Traje de baño**
Bathing suit

146 **Traje de etiqueta**
Formal dress

147 **Traje largo**
Evening dress

148 **Transporte de locura**
Fit of madness

149 **Tras de**
Behind, after, beside

150 **Trastos de cocina**
Kitchen utensils

151 **Trastos de pescar**
Fishing tackle

152 **Tratar con**
To have dealings with

153 **Tratar de**
To try to, to treat of, to deal with

154 **Tratar en**
To deal in

155 **Tratarse de**
To be a question of

156 **¡Trato hecho!**
It's a deal!

157 **Tren correo**
Mail train

158 **Tren de aterrizaje**
Landing gear

159 **Tren de carga**
Freight train

160 **Tren de recreo**
Excursion train

161 **Tren de servicio directo**
Through train

162 **Tren expreso**
Express train

163 **Tren mixto**
Freight and passenger train

164 **Tren rápido**
Through train

165 **Tronar los dedos**
To snap one's fingers

166 **Tropezar con**
To meet, come across, encounter

167 **Tubo de ensayo**
Test tube

168 **Tubo de escape**
Tail pipe

U

1 **Un buen pasar**
Enough to live on

2 **Un día de éstos**
One of these (fine) days

3 **Un día sí y otro no**
Every other day

4 **Un día sí y un día no**
Every other day

5 **Un hervidero de gente**
A swarm of people

6 **Un no sé qué**
Something indefinable

7 **Un nudo en la garganta**
A lump in the throat

8 **Un par de**
A couple of

9 **Un par de pantalones**
A pair of trousers

10 **Un rato desagradable**
A hard time

11 **Un tanto**
Somewhat

12 **Una buena carcajada**
A hearty laugh

13 **Una infinidad de**
A large number of

14 **Una mala pasada**
A mean trick

*15 **Una negativa rotunda**
A flat denial

16 **Una negativa terminante**
A flat denial

17 **Una que otra vez**
Once in a while

18 **Una y otra vez**
More than once, over and
over again

19 **Unas cuantas** (or **Unos cuantos**)
A few

20 **Uno a la vez**
One at a time

21 **Uno por uno**
One by one

22 **Unos a otros**
Each other

23 **Unos pocos**
A few

24 **Urna electoral**
Ballot box

V

1 **Vajilla de plata**
Silverware

2 **Valer la pena**
To be worthwhile
Ex.: **No vale la pena.**
It's not worth the trouble.

3 **Valer más**
To be better

4 **Valer por**
To be worth

5 **Valerse de**
To make use of

6 **Valor nominal**
Small value, insignificant

7 **Varias veces**
Several times

8 **Varita de virtud**
Magic wand

9 **Vender al menudeo**
To sell at retail

10 **Venir a las manos**
To come to blows

11 **Venir a menos**
To decay, decline

12 **Venir a parar**
To turn out to be,
to end up (as)

13 **Venir a** (or **al**) **pelo**
To come at right moment, to
suit perfectly, to be opportune

14 **Venir a ser**
To turn out to be

15 **Venir bien**
To suit

16 **Venir en**
To agree to

17 **Venir sobre**
To fall upon

18 **Venirse abajo**
To fall down, collapse, fail

19 **Venta pública**
Auction

20 **Ver de** (or **Ver que**)
To try to, see to it that

21 **Ver visiones**
To have false impressions
or fantasies, to "see" things

22 **Verse obligado a**
To be obliged to or forced to

23 **Vestido de**
Dressed in

24 **¡Vete a bañar!**
Go jump in the lake!
(See SEC. III for additional
similar idiomatic expressions.)

25 **Vidriera de colores**
Stained glass window

26 Violación de un compromiso
Breach of promise

27 Visita domiciliaria
Police inspection of a house,
or home call by a social worker

28 Visto que
Whereas, considering that

*29 Vivir de sus uñas
To live by stealing

30 Voltear la espalda
To turn one's back

31 Volver a (+ inf.)
To do - - - again

*32 Volver a las andadas
To fall back into old habits

33 Volver corriendo
To hurry back

34 Volver en sí
To come to, regain consciousness

35 Volver loco
To drive crazy

36 Volver por
To return for, to defend

37 Volverse atrás
To go back, back out, go back
on one's word

38 Volverse loco
To go crazy

39 Voz alta
Aloud

Y

1 Y así sucesivamente
And so on, et cetera

2 Y pico
(A) little more

3 ¿Y qué?
So what?

4 ¿Y si?
What if - - -?

5 Ya es hora de
It's time to

6 Ya es tarde.
It's too late now.

7 Ya merito.
It won't be long now.

8 Ya mero
Very soon, just about to - - -

9 ¡Ya lo creo!
I should say so! Yes, of course.

10 Ya no
No longer

11 Ya no sopla
To be no good, of no use as - - -

12 Ya que
Since, although

13 Ya se acabó.
It is all over.

14 Ya se ve.
Of course; It is clear.

15 Ya voy.
I am coming.

16 Yacimiento de petróleo
Oil field

17 Yema del dedo
Finger tip

18 Yeso blanco
Whitewash

19 Yeso mate
Plaster of Paris

SECTION II
IDIOMS — ENGLISH TO SPANISH

This section gives the English equivalents of **only** the Spanish idioms of SECTION I and does not attempt to give Spanish equivalents for the vast number of English idioms and idiomatic expressions in common usage. Also it should be noted that SECTION I may give only one way of saying something, whereas the English equivalent could be expressed in several ways in Spanish. For example, there is in SECTION I only one idiomatic expression for "maybe" (or "perhaps") and for "hummingbird". In these two instances, a footnote is provided to give other single-word equivalents. Such footnotes are, however, rare exceptions. There are many cases in which single words may be used in place of idioms or phrases. Hence the unavoidable limitations of this section on English equivalents must be given due consideration. However, SECTION II is especially useful when one cannot recall an idiom of SECTION I, but remembers the English equivalent of SECTION II.

Some of the English entries of this section are single words, but the Spanish equivalents are idiomatic expressions of more than one word.

Strict letter-by-letter alphabetizing is utilized in this section; whereas in SECTION I, alphabetizing follows the word order, i.e., first word, second word, etc.

Regarding the use of parentheses ( ), see SECTION I.

A

about: A 163, A 234, A 255, C 155, R 33
about that: P 184
about the first of - - - - -: A 111
about the middle of - - - - -: A 79
above: P 190
above all: A 272, P 214, S 133
abroad: E 90
absolutely: D 207
absolutely (<u>not</u>): E 61
(to) accomplish: LL12
according to the customs of the period: A 243
according to the rules: C 91
across: A 147, D 228
across country: A 9
across the sea: A 258
(to) act a fool: H 38, H 92
(to) act as: H 31, S 84

(to) act as if: H 28
actually: D 289
(to) act without restraint: S139
adhesive tape: T 21
(to) adjourn a meeting: L 37
admission fee: C 183
(to) admit a person is right: D 47
adult: M 39
adults only: S 137
afloat: A 33
after: T 149
after a few months (etc.): A 71
after all: A 29, D 295, E 134
again: D 177, D 250, O 21
against: E 79
against all odds: C 141
against the grain: A 17
(to) agree: D 46, E 223, Q 40
agreed: A 227

(to) agree to: Q 40, V 16
ahead: P 200
(to) aim at: P 160
aimlessly: A 54
(to) aim very high: P 108
air mail: C 146
alarm clock: R 23
a little more: Y 2
all along: D 285
all around: A 52
all at once: D 229, D 234, D 236
all by oneself (himself): P 264
all day: T 113
all goes well: T 121
all joking aside: B 29, F 18
all kinds of: T 109
all of a sudden: D 125, D 208
all over: P 268, P 272
all over the world: P 270
all right: E 217
all right then: P 308
all sides: P 272
all that is possible: T 120
all the time: A 6, T 116
all the while: E 178
all together: E 104
all year round: T 112
almost: P 256
alone: A 133
along, along side of: A 65
along with: J 10
a lot of: A 74
aloud: E 159, V 39
although: B 13, P 314, S 89, Y 12
aluminum foil: H 130
among: P 216
(to) amuse: H 46
and so: D 171, D 221
and so on: Y 1
(to) anger: D 69
angina pectoris: A 271
(to) annoy: D 43
anteater: O 16
anyhow: A 299, D 226
anything at all: C 163
anyway: A 211, D 225, E 80

any way you look at it: A 142
apiece: C 8
(to) apologize: D 85
apparently: A 226, P 244
applesauce: C 111
(to) approve: D 25
approximately: C 155
apropos: A 112
arm in arm: D 116
armor plate: P 124
around (about): A 202, A 234,
      A 255
around here: A 285, P 189
around the corner: A 59, A 60
(to) arouse one's suspicions: D 88
(to) arouse pity or sorrow: D 51
(to) arrest: E 14
as: A 80, S 54
as a general rule: P 260
as a (bad) habit: D 247
as a joke: E 69
as a last resort: C 108
as a matter of fact: E 130
as a pledge: E 124
as a result (of): A 15, D 210
as a rule: P 240
as a whole: E 78
as far as I'm concerned: P 249
as follows: A 16, C 107
as for: E 82
as for the rest (of us): P 234
aside from that: A 281
aside from this: P 234
as if: C 103
as if it were: C 105
as if nothing had happened:
      C 104
as is: A 297
as I understand it: A 86
(to) ask about: P 280
(to) ask a question (or questions):
      H 62
(to) ask to dance: S 5
as little as possible: L 53
as long as: S 97

as much as: T 14
as of: A 97
as proof of: E 124
as someone said: C 90
as soon as: A 293, A 297, E 81,
　　L 62, T 13
as soon as possible: C 166, L 52
(to) assume responsibility: C 45
as the crow flies: A 157
as time goes on: A 268
as usual: C 89, C 106, S 110
as well as: A 291
as you like: A 58
at about: A 26, C 88
at about - - - - - (re time): A 208
at all: D 273
at all costs: A 138, A 144
at all hours: A 20
at all times: A 139
at an early date: E 99
at another's expense: D 145
at any cost: C 180
at any moment: D 231
at any rate: C 99, D 132, D 225
　　D 226
at any time: A 139
at arm's length: A 150
at a short distance: A 108
at bottom: E 91
at dawn, daybreak: A 110, A 191
at dusk (nightfall): A 192
at every turn: A 5
at first: A 231
at full length: A 65
at full sail: A 23, A 141, A 145
at full speed (or greatest speed):
　　A 23, A 140, A 141, A 143
at hand: A 73
at hard labor: A 235
at heart: E 91
at home: E 72
at last: A 51, A 209, A 211, P 223,
　　P 274
at (the) least: A 218, C 94, M 59,
　　P 238
at length: P 220

at (the) most: A 67, A 69
at night: A 50, D 176, P 229
at nightfall: A 192, A 195
atomic bomb: B 24
at once: A 187, A 215, A 232,
　　D 196, D 237, D 289, E 89,
　　E 141
at one's side: A 216
at one stroke: D 237
at one time: A 152, D 237
at present: A 230, P 225
at random: A 42, A 54, A 193
at retail: A 204, A 219, A 237
at sunset: A 43
(to) attend to personally: T 135
at that time: A 53, E 66
at the end: A 209
at the last moment: A 148
at the mercy of (or expense of):
　　A 85
at the most: A 69
at the oar: A 235
at the present time: E 105
at the rate of: A 127
at the request of: A 39
at the same time: A 56, A 220,
　　D 188, E 178
at the very latest: A 77
at times: A 125, A 153
at twilight: A 225
at whatever cost: A 138
at what price: A 14
at wholesale: A 217, P 236
at will: A 58
at worst: A 67
At your service: A 136, S 83
auction: V 19
automotive transmission: C 17
(the) average person: E 42
(to) avoid someone: D 31
awaiting: E 96

B

baby grand piano: P 105

back and forth: D 113

back door: P 306

(to) back out: E 35, V 37

(to) back up: D 56, I 24

backward(s): A 236, H 102

bad habits: M 6

bad temper: M 2

bad tricks or habits: M 6

ballot box: U 24

bankruptcy proceedings: P 130

(a) bargain: D 178

(to) bark up the wrong tree: A 3

basic material: M 38

(The) basis of it is - - - - -: E 194

bathing suit: T 145

bathroom: C 169

(to) be a bore: S 78

(to) be a buff: S 65

(to) be about to: E 211, E 273

beachhead: C 2

(to) be adrift: I 25

(to) be a fan: S 65

(to) be afraid of (or to): T 68

(to) be against: E 255, P 178

(to) be a good housekeeper: S 81

(to) be agreed to: Q 41

(to) be ahead: LL 19

(to) be alert: E 210, P 171

(to) be all right, O.K.: E 217

(to) be alluring: T 53

(to) be a load off one's mind: Q 57

(to) be an early riser: S 77

(to) be anxious to: N 84

(to) be a part of: F 10

(to) be a question of: T 155

(to) bear false witness: L 35

(to) bear in mind: T 73

(to) be arrogant: T 70

(to) be ashamed: T 85

(to) beat around the bush: A 267,
    A 269

beaten path: C 39

(to) be at the end of one's rope or
    resources: E 252

(to) beat time: LL 15

(to) be attractive: T 53

beautifully: A 64

beauty parlor: S 29

(to) be a wallflower: P 125

(to) be away from home: E 265

(to) be back: E 234, E 241

(to) be becoming: C 10, Q 42, S 61

(to) be better: V 3

(to) be between the devil and the
    deep blue sea: E 263

(to) be beyond help or repair:
    N 73

(to) be born lucky: N 1

(to) be broke: E 219

because: N 62

because of: C 119

because of things or events beyond
    my control: P 191

because of which: P 241

(to) be cautious: E 279

(to) be coaxed: H 88

(to) be cold: T 51

(to) become: LL 9

(to) become confused: H 99

(to) become effective: E 172

(to) become firmly fixed: E 23

(to) become overcast (cloudy):
    C 70

(to) be comfortable: E 209

(to) be completely filled up: E 224

(to) be concerned about or for:
    P 284

(to) be confined to bed: G 14

(to) be contented: E 209

(to) be courageous: T 76

(to) be crowded: E 224

(to) be cruel: N 69

(to) be cultured: S 72

(to) be deeply involved: E 272

(to) be disappointed: LL 22, Q 45

(to) be disconcerting: D 57

(to) be dull: N 74

(to) be eager to: T 42

(to) be (an) early riser: S 77

beef: C 49

(to) be eloquent: T 43
(to) be exhausted: N 51
(to) be expecting: E 256
(to) be fed: D 21
(to) be fed up: E 282, E 283
(to) be fed up with: E 267
(to) be filled up: E 268
(to) be flush (even with): E 276
(to) be fond of: E 214
(to) be fooled: LL 22
(to) be forced to: V 22
before: A 274
before dark: D 134
beforehand: C 129
before you get to: M 21
(to) be funny: T 54
(to) begin: E 33, P 168, R 40
beginning on: A 97
(to) begin running: E 1
(to) begin to understand: I 23
(to) be glad to: T 55
(to) be going on: E 247
(to) be good enough to: T 57
(to) be good for: S 86
(to) be good for nothing: N 65
(to) be harsh: S 80
(to) be haughty: T 70
behind: A 303, D 297, T 149
behind closed doors: A 115
behind one's back: A 27
behind the scenes: E 174
behold: H 125
(to) be hot: T 36
(to) be hungry: T 56
(to) be ill-tempered: T 67
(to) be in a bad humor: E 271
(to) be in a good humor: E 249
(to) be in a hurry: E 233, T 74
(to) be in a jam: E 258
(to) be in charge of: E 208, E 261
(to) be in compliance with: E 225
(to) be in conflict with: E 255
(to) be in danger: E 254
(to) be indebted to: E 248
(to) be indispensable: S 68

(to) be in favor of: E 275
(to) be in gear: E 262
(to) be in good condition: E 245
(to) be in good health: E 218, S 110
(to) be in great danger: T 63
(to) be in infancy: E 253
(to) be in jail: E 244
(to) be in labor: E 231
(to) be in mourning: E 226, E 228
(to) be in need of: H 40
(to) be in one's right mind: E 281
(to) be in order: E 216
(to) be inspired: E 260
(to) be in the mood: E 238, E 260
(to) be in the same boat: E 250
(to) be in the way: E 235
(to) be in trouble: E 258
(to) be irritable: S 80
(to) be jealous: T 38
(to) be jilted: D 92
(to) be judge of: S 67
(to) be just about out of money: E 264
(to) be left alone: E 230
(to) be left in the lurch: Q 45
(to) believe: T 72
(to) be long (in doing): T 17
(to) be lost from view: P 98
below: A 16
(to) be lucky: T 83, T 107
(to) be mistaken: E 259
(to) be nauseated: T 32
(to) be nearly - - - - - (o'clock):
    P 134
beneath: D 251
(to) be necessary: S 71
(to) be no good: Y 11
(to) be obliged to: V 22
(to) be obvious: S 30
(to) be of no account: S 79
(to) be of no use: Y 11
(to) be of the same opinion: D 46
(to) be on duty: E 236
(to) be one's own affair: C 147
(to) be one's turn: T 106, T 107
(to) be on good terms with: A 164

(to) be on intimate terms with: T 39

(to) be on one's last legs: E 252

(to) be on relief: R 10

(to) be on sale: E 239

(to) be on the alert: E 210, E 279

(to) be on the lookout for: E 210

(to) be on the road: E 240

(to) be on the way: E 246

(to) be on unfriendly terms with: E 280

(to) be on vacation: E 237

(to) be opportune: V 13

(to) be opposed to: E 255

(to) be out of a job: M 54

(to) be out of luck: E 229

(to) be out of resources: E 252

(to) be out of sorts: A 264, N 28

(to) be out of the house: E 265

(to) be passing through: E 232

(to) be perfectly even: E 276

(to) be pleased with: Q 39

(to) be pleased with oneself: P 3

(to) be prone to: E 214

(to) be proud of: P 10

(to) be (a) question of: T 155

(to) be rejected: D 92

(to) be relieved of: Q 57

(to) be repulsive: S 78

(to) be required by custom: S 68

(to) be responsible for: H 87

(to) be ridiculous: H 38

(to) be right: A 265, T 79

(to) be running: I 17

(to) be safe: E 207

(to) be satisfied: E 283

(to) be seldom at home: S 73

(to) be shy: T 85

beside: A 62, T 149

beside oneself: F 21

besides (to boot): D 191, S 131

besides that: A 281

(to) be sleepy: T 82

(to) be soaked through: E 270

(to) be socially important: S 72

(to) be sopping wet: E 270

(to) be sorry for someone: P 100

(to) be stingy: S 66

(to) be strong: T 76

best seller: D 167, E 290

(to) be stubborn: S 70

(to) be stuffed: E 282

(to) be stupid: N 74

(to) be successful: S 22, T 50

(to) be sulky: T 71

(to) be surprised: LL 22

(to) be terribly sorry: S 63

(to) be the goat: P 6

(to) be the object of scandal: S 75

(to) be thirsty: T 81

(to) be ticklish: T 40

(to) be to blame: T 59

(to) be too complicated: P 77

(to) be too good: P 76

(to) be to one's advantage: C 145

(to) be traveling: E 240

better late than never: M 35

better yet: M 55

between: P 216

between the devil and the deep blue sea: E 175

(to) be unable to cope with: N 20

(to) be understood: Q 41

(to) be unfaithful: P 144

(to) be unlucky: E 278

(to) be unwilling to do it: N 55

(to) be up-to-date: E 212, E 213, E 246

(to) be up to oneself: C 147

(to) be used as: S 84

(to) be used for: S 86

(to) be used to - - - - -: T 58

(to) be very angry: E 10

(to) be very eager to (or for): R 1

(to) be very difficult: C 156

(to) be very sorry: E 221, T 69

(to) be very thin: E 269

(to) be very unclear: P 77

(to) be violating the law: E 266

(to) be waiting for: E 256

(to) be (a) wallflower: P 125

(to) be wary: P 171

(to) be well: S 110

(to) be well-informed: E 212, E 213, E 246

(to) be well off: E 242

(to) be willing: E 243

(to) be windy: H 10, H 20, H 124

(to) be without a partner (or companion): E 230

(to) be worse off: E 274

(to) be worth: V 4

(to) be worthless: N 64

(to) be worthwhile: M 60, V 2

(to) be wrong: E 259, N 72

(to) be - - - - - years old: T 31

beyond: M 24

bill (legislative): P 298

billiard (pool) cue: T 4

bill of exchange: L 29

bill of fare: L 48

bill of sale: C 55

bird of prey: A 308

birth certificate: C 71

birth control: C 144, L 46

black coffee: C 15

(to) blame: D 27, E 9, E 13

blind alley: C 29

blindly: A 12, A 94

block of ice: T 25

(to) block the door: I 4

bloodshed: D 281, E 36

blotting paper: P 27

(to) blush: P 170

boarding house: C 57

(to) boast of: H 43, P 10

bomb shelter: R 17

bookkeeper: T 26

bookkeeping: T 27

(to) book passage: R 32

(to) border on: P 107

(to) borrow: P 78

(to) bother about: M 73

brake drum: T 12

(to) brand as: M 82

brand new: E 171, N 91

breach of promise: V 26

(to) break camp: L 34

(to) break into: F 11

(to) break into pieces: H 59

(to) break one's word: F 4, P 116

(to) break the news: D 45

(to) break the thread of a story: C 152

(to) bridge a gap: LL 10

bridgehead: C 3

(to) bring a lawsuit: E 170

(to) bring charges or a lawsuit against: P 163

(to) bring out into the open: S 7

(to) bring up to date: P 140

brown paper: P 23

Brussels sprouts: C 84

bulky: D 118

bulletin board: T 2

bullfight: C 149

bullring: P 129

Bully for you!: A 298

(to) bump into each other: D 101

(to) burn down: Q 47

(the) burning question: L 3

(to) burn midnight oil: Q 48

(to) burst with laughter: R 35

(to) bury: D 72

business man: H 134

but: S 121

But I already told you: S 96

by accident: P 182, P 193

by all means: A 138, A 142, D 226, S 106

by chance: A 193, P 193

by day: D 134

by degrees: D 146

by dint of: A 35

by ear: D 179

by foot: A 103

by force (of): A 35, A 46

by freight: P 192

by guess: A 93, A 240

by hand: A 73

by heart: D 169
by installments: A 105
by itself: D 194
by just shouting: A 118
by means of: P 246
by mistake: S 114
by myself: P 248
by nature: D 222
by night: D 176
by no means: D 174, D 175
by oneself: P 263, P 265
by pure chance: D 201
by rail: P 222
by retail: P 237
by return mail: A 158
by sheer force: A 117
by sight: A 93
by the day: P 205
by the looks of: P 244
by the minute: D 200
by the roots: D 204
by the way: A 112, D 188, E 176
by two's: D 138
by wholesale: E 103, P 236
by word of mouth: D 183, D 248

C

(to) call a spade a spade: A 224,
    LL 2
(to) call at a port: H 39
(to) call on the phone: LL 3
(to) call the roll: P 58
capital letter: L 30
capital punishment: P 84, P 85
carpet sweeper: E 186
(to) carry away: C 45
(to) carry out: D 15, LL 13, LL 20
(to) carry through: LL 12
carving: L 16
cash: A 197
cash book: L 41
cash down, cash and carry: A 200
cash register: C 20

(to) cast a shadow: H 69
(to) catch cold: C 82
(to) catch fire: C 83
(to) cause distress or grief to: D 22
(to) cause extra work: D 68
(to) cause pain or worry: H 55
(to) cause sorrow: D 57
(x) cents off: R 7
certainly not: C 78
chain of misfortunes: R 45
change: D 314, M 77, M 78
(to) change one's mind: C 32
(to) change the subject: C 34
charcoal: C 44
charge account: C 172, C 173
(to) charge on account: C 47
(to) chase after a woman: A 270
chattels: B 15
(to) chatter constantly: H 9
(to) cheat: D 34
checkpoint: P 315
(to) cheer up: D 10
(to) choose: O 13
Christmas: P 64
cigarette paper: P 24
circular (handbill): P 31
(to) clarify: P 147
clearly: A 63, A 95
clear profit: L 47
(to) clear the table: L 36, Q 56
(to) clear up: P 147
close attention: S 154
closer: M 20
close to: A 123, C 69
clothing store: C 22
(The) coast is not clear: H 117
cock and bull story: C 175
coffin: C 21
(to) collide with: D 101
(to) collapse: V 18
(to) come across: E 165, T 166
(to) come at the right moment:
    V 13
(to) come from: S 74
Come in: P 65

(to) come out ahead: S 26
(to) come out as desired: S 156
(to) come our poorly: S 27
(to) come out well: Q 38, S 22, S 156
(to) come to: V 34
(to) come to a boil: S 138
(to) come to an agreement: P 172
(to) come to blows: V 10
(to) come to know: LL 8
(to) come to pass: LL 9
Come to the point: D 267, I 16
come what may: S 151
(to) commit an error: I 9
(to) complain loudly: P 146
(to) complain of: Q 46
(to) complete: D 15, D 33
completely: D 204, P 195
(to) compliment: E 11, E 25
computer: C 23
concerning: R 33
(to) conclude: S 10
concretely: E 76
confidentially: A 221
(to) confront: E 167
consciously: A 130
(to) conscript: E 18
consequently: D 210, P 197, P 198
(to) consider: P 43, T 44, T 72,
    T 131
(to) consider as: D 60
(to) consider as done: D 62
considering that: V 28
continually: A 4, P 226
continuously: D 213
control panel: T 3
(to) coordinate: P 152
copyright: D 280
cornerstone: P 109
counterfeit: M 76
(to) count on: C 139
(a) couple of: U 8
course of study: P 123
(to) court: H 48
courtroom: S 15
covered with: C 160

cowhide: C 176
crawling: A 36
(to) crawl out of difficulty: S 20
credit card: T 19
(to) creep or crawl: A 263
cross country: A 9
crowd: R 24
crowded: D 115
crow's foot wrinkles: P 71
crude: E 129
crude oil: P 103
cube of sugar: T 89
currency: M 75
curriculum: P 123
(to) curse: E 27
(to) cut class: H 60
(to) cut into strips: H 66
Cut it out!: Q 7

D

(the) daily grind: L 10
dandelion: D 309
(to) dance without music: B 1
dating from: D 287
(to) dawn: R 41
day after day: D 305
day after tomorrow: P 51
daybreak: A 191
(to) daydream: E 251, S 144
days of old: D 306
(to) deal in: T 154
(to) deal with: T 153
death certificate: P 48
(to) decay: V 11
deceitfully: A 146, D 162
deceitful story told to get money:
    E 43
(to) deceive: P 144
(to) decide: T 138
(to) decide upon: O 13
(to) decline: V 11
(to) deduce: S 10
(to) defend: V 36
(to) delay: D 49

delivery truck: C 40
(to) demolish: E 22
(to) depart: S 23
derby hat: S 141
(to) destroy: D 8, D 9
Devil's advocate: A 159
(to) devour: E 34
diagonally: A 238
(to) die: E 285, P 52
dining car: C 80
(to) disappoint: P 81
(to) discharge (a patient): D 19
(to) discriminate against: H 41
(to) disembark: S 31
(to) dismiss: D 20
(to) displease: C 11, N 19
(to) disappoint: P 81
(to) "ditch": D 31
(to) do again: H 32, V 31
(to) dock the wages: R 8
(to) dodge: S 9
(to) do it again: T 142
Don't be like that. N 37
Don't handle the merchandise.
　　S 93
Don't hurry. N 58
Don't mention it: D 173, N 32
Don't tell me that: Q 55
Don't worry: N 59, N 60
Don't worry about it. N 75
(to) do one's best: H 52, P 166
(to) do over: H 32, H 58
double-entry bookkeeping: P 49
(to) doubt: P 149
(to) do without: P 63
downhill: C 178
downstream: A 178, C 117, R 36
down the street: C 27
(to) draft: E 18
draft (money): L 29
draft beer: C 72
drawbridge: P 302
(to) draw lots: E 20, E 24
(to) dream of: S 143
dressed in: V 23

(to) drift: I 25
(to) drink: T 127
drinkable water: A 175
(to) drink down: E 34
(to) drink too much: A 256, E 59
(to) drive crazy: V 35
driving force: F 22
(to) drop: D 260
(to) drop out: D 94, D 262
(to) drop out of sight: P 98
dry dock: D 316
dry goods store: C 22
dry measure: M 52
dunce: T 141
during the week: A 79, E 177

E

each one: C 5
each other: E 56, U 22
each time: A 6
(the) earliest possible: L 49
early in (time): A 111
(to) earn a living: G 3
earthquake: T 24
either: E 57
either of the two: C 164
electric outlet: T 123
electric plug: T 123
electric razor: M 14
emergency hospital: C 60
(to) emphasize: D 71, H 34
(to) emulate: S 53
Encore!: O 20
(to) encounter: T 166
(to) endanger: P 142
(to) end up as: V 12
(to) end up by (doing something):
　　A 162
(to) enhance: D 71
Enjoy your meal!: B 31
enough to live on: U 1
entirely free: L 47
equally: A 214
equal to or up to: C 116

especially: A 272, E 95, E 120,
S 133
(to) esteem highly: T 47
et cetera: Y 1
even dozen: D 321
even if: A 305
evening dress: T 147
even so: A 299, A 304
even though: A 305, N 15
even with: A 124
ever since: D 286
everybody: T 114
everybody who: T 115
every day: T 122
everyone: T 117
every other day: C 7, U 3, U 4
everything else: T 119
every time: T 110
everywhere: E 147, P 268, P 272
evidently: P 244
evil eye: M 4
exactly as: S 54
exactly as desired: A 99
exactly the opposite: T 118
(to) exasperate (someone): S 8
except for: S 94, S 95
excess baggage: E 289
excessively: S 129
exclusive of: S 103
excursion train: T 160
Excuse me: C 122
(to) execute: P 60
executioner: E 37
express train: T 162
(to) extend condolences
to or for: D 24
(to) extol: P 150
extra: D 209
extremely: C 115
eye witness: T 91, T 92

F

(to) face: D 3, H 42, H 67
face down: B 20

face up: B 21
(the) fact is: E 41
faculty of a school: C 177
(to) fail: D 92, S 27, V18
fair: T 6
fair complexion: T 93
fair play: J 4
fairyland: T 96
(to) fall back into old habits: V 32
(to) fall down: I 27, V 18
(to) fall ill: C 12
(to) fall into an error: I 9
(to) fall to one's lot: T 107
(to) fall upon: V 17
farther away: M 24
farther on: M 22
fast asleep: P 292
(to) feed: D 21
feed reel: B 18, C 51
(to) feel feverish: S 64
(to) feel like: T 52
(to) feel O.K.: E 277
(to) feel sorry for: T 64
(x) feet long: P 113
(x) feet tall: P 112
(to) feign: H 64
feigned illness: C 24
(to) feign illness: H 49
(a) few: U 19, U 23
(a) few lines: C 170
(a) few words: C 171
(to) fib: E 21
field glasses: A 273
(to) file a complaint: P 167
(to) fill an order: S 157
filming of a movie: R 39
finally: A 194, E 100, P 223, P 273,
P 274
(to) find fault with: P 145, P 157
(to) find no way out: N 31
(to) find the right way to do
something: D 87
fine weather: T 94
fingerprints: H 139
finger tip: Y 17

fire insurance: S 55
fireplug: B 23
fireproof: A 114
fireworks: F 17
firm name: R 6
first aid: P 289
first aid station: P 313
first of all: A 272
fishing boat: B 36
fishing tackle: A 280, T 151
(to) fit badly: C 11
fit of anger: A 289, I 5
fit of madness: T 148
(to) fit well: C 10, S 60
(to) fix one's eyes on: P 160
(to) flash by: P 53
flashlight: L 64
(a) flat denial: U 15, U 16
(to) flatter: D 16, D 39, E 11, E 25
flimsy fabric: T 22
(to) flirt (with): E 215, H 26
floating dock: D 317
flush with: A 32, A 124
folk music: M 90, M 91
(to) follow in footsteps: S 53
fond of (or friend of): A 260, A 261
(to) fool: H 29
(to) fool oneself: H 94
(to) foot the bill: P 8
for a change: P 41
for and against: E 126
for certain: D 215
foreground: P 287
foreign born: E 292
foreign office: M 69
foreign trade: C 87
forever: P 38
for example: P 208
(to) forget on purpose: E 5
Forget it: N 75
for hire: A 254
formal: D 143
formal dress: T 146
(to) form a line: H 27
for now: P 185

for one purpose or another: P 40
for rent: A 254, S 39
for sale: S 52
for some reason: P 186
for some time now: D 108
for sure: D 215
for that reason: P 217, P 219
for the first time: P 257
for the last time: P 273
for the present: P 199, P 212
for the sake of: E 116
for the time being: D 172, P 185,
  P 210, P 239
for want of: A 28
forward: H 101
For what use?: P 34
foster father: P 1
foul play: J 5
(to) founder: I 26
(to) frame someone: C 137
frankly: A 63, S 115, S 118
free: E 106
freedom to act: C 53
free entry: P 305
free of charge: D 114
free port: P 307
free reign: A 128
free trade: L 40
freight and passenger train: T 163
freight train: T 159
frequently: A 4, C 120
fresh water: A 173
fried eggs: H 141
(to) frighten: D 38
frivolous: L 45
from across the sea: A 149
from a distance: D 155, D 288
from afar: D 288
from bad to worse: D 158
from beginning to end: D 127
from life: D 271
from nature: D 271
from now on: D 106, D 112, D 149,
  D 284, E 62
from one side to the other: D 185

from that time on: D 111
from the beginning: D 285, D 291
from then on: D 105
from the outside: P 224
from the rear: P 204
from time to time: A 125, D 223
from today on: A 98
from top to bottom: D 110
(to) froth at the mouth: E 10
(to) frown: F 14, F 16
full authority: C 53
full blast: A 76
full-fledged: H 126
full-length mirror: E 197
full of: C 160
full to the brim: LL 11
fully: A 34
(to) furnish all the data: F 1
furthermore: M 25

G

gasoline station: E 205
generally: P 232, P 235
(to) get along well with: LL 21,
    Q 38
(to) get down to cases: I 16
(to) get drunk: P 114
(to) get fat: E 6
(to) get going: P 154
(to) get late: H 98
(to) get late in the evening: H 97
Get lost!: V 24
(to) get married: C 142
(to) get oneself in a mess: M 64
(to) get on the train: S 148
(to) get out of a difficulty: S 24
Get out of here!: L 22, Q 58
(to) get ready to leave: H 50
(to) get tangled up: H 99
(to) get the blame: P 6
(to) get the blame unjustly: C 46
(to) get the point: C 13
(to) get to be: LL 8
(to) get to one's feet: P 173

(to) get to sleep: C 131
(to) get up: P 173, P 180
(to) get up on the wrong side of the
    bed: L 39
(to) get used to: H 83
(to) get well: P 169
(to) get worse: S 149
ginger ale: C 73
gingerbread: O 14, P 17
(to) give account: D 70
(to) give a party: D 82
(to) give a report on: D 17
(to) give a scare: P 83
(to) give birth: D 7
(to) give cause for: D 54
(to) give good results: S 156
(to) give it up: D 91
given name: N 86, N 87
(to) give opportunity (or occasion)
    to: D 59
(to) give regards: D 53
(to) give someone the run around:
    D 49
(to) give something up for lost:
    E 32
(to) give thanks: D 50
(to) give to: D 3
(to) give up: D 97
(to) give up (or get rid of)
    something: Q 59
gladly: C 121, D 123, D 249
(to) glance (off): P 79
(to) glance over: D 80
(to) gnash one's teeth: R 13
(to) go arm in arm: I 22
(to) go back: V 37
(to) go back on one's word: E 35,
    V 37
(to) go blind: P 96
(to) go cautiously: C 35
(to) go crazy: P 92, V 38
(to) go downtown: I 15
God willing: D 315
(to) go fishing: I 20
(to) go for a drive: P 67

(to) go for a sail: D 74
(to) go halves (50-50): I 13
(to) go horseback riding: P 68
goings and comings: I 2
Go jump in the lake!: V 24
Go lay an egg!: V 24
goldfish: C 50
gold standard: P 74
Good afternoon: B 34
Good appetite!: B 31
Goodbye: A 78, H 110, H 111
Good day: B 35
good fellow: B 33
good looking: B 11, D 120
Good luck: Q 20
Good morning: B 35
Good night: B 34
(to) go on a journey: H 75
(to) go on a spree: A 266, I 19
(to) go on foot: I 14
(to) go on vacation: I 31
goose bumps (or pimples): C 48
(to) go out for a good time: E 29
(to) go out of style: P 55
(to) go out to meet: S 21
(to) go over carefully: P 61
Go peddle your papers! V 24
(to) go shopping: I 18
(to) grab: E 14
grade crossing: P 70
gradually: P 132
grand jury: J 11
grand piano: P 104
grandstand: G 11
(to) grasp: E 17
(to) grasp a hand: E 287
gratis: D 114
grizzly bear: O 18
gross weight: P 101
ground floor: P 119, P 126
(to) grow late: H 97
grown up: H 126
(to) guess right: D 30
(to) gulp down: B 6

H

(to) hail from: S 74
half-done: A 82
half-way (to a place): A 81
Halt!: P 59
handbill: P 31
hand grenade: G 12
hand-made: A 73
handsome man: B 30
haphazardly: A 54

happy-go-lucky: CH 2
harbor pilot: P 278
hard-boiled eggs: H 140
hard cash: D 313
hard knot: N 89
hardly ever: C 63
hard of hearing: A 246, C 153,
    M 53
(a) hard time: U 10
hard water: A 169
hard-working: M 94
hatless and coatless: E 84
(to) have a bad time: S 152
(to) have a big mouth: T 61
(to) have a birthday: C 181
(to) have a finger in everything:
    E 257
Have a good day: Q 21
(to) have a good time: P 62
(to) have a hangover: E 222, E 227
(to) have an affair with: E 168
(to) have an illness: E 220
(to) have a screw loose: F 6
(to) have a sore throat: D 322, T 66
(to) have charge of: E 261
(to) have connections (or dealings)
    with someone: R 46
(to) have contact with a person:
    T 80
(to) have dealings with: T 152
(to) have discomfort: E 220
(to) have dislike for: T 86

(to) have false impressions or fantasies: V 21

(to) have influence with someone: T 35

(to) have in mind: T 45

(to) have in sight: T 28

(to) have just (done something): A 161

(to) have little sense: F 6

(to) have no alternative: N 68

(to) have nothing to do with: N 70

(to) have no way out: N 68

(to) have on: T 144

(to) have one's own way: S 28

(to) have on the tip of one's tongue: T 46

(to) have physical strength: T 37

(to) have received a letter: T 28

(to) have the blues: T 71

(to) have the lead: LL 19

(to) have the misfortune to - - -: T 62

(to) have time off: T 84

(to) have to (do something): T 77

(to) have to do with: T 78

hay fever: C 65

headache: D 323

heads or tails: A 181, A 182

(to) head towards: H 68

He almost died: P 256

health department: S 35

heaps: A 90

(to) hear about: O 8

(to) hear a piece of news early or for the first time: D 282

(to) hear from: R 11

hearing aid: A 279

hearsay: D 180

heart attack: A 301

heart failure: A 300

(to) hear that: O 7

heart trouble: E 166

(a) hearty laugh: U 12

height of folly: C 85

He is in favor of doing it: E 46

Hello!: Q 32

(to) help: D 44

Help yourself: S 122

hence: P 215

Here!: A 136

hereafter: E 109

here below: D 224

Here is - - - : H 125

hideous face: C 43

high rank: D 130

highway: C 36, C 38

(to) hinder: H 54

(to) hit or hit upon: D 26

(to) hit at a slant: P 79

hit or miss: A 240, CH 2

(to) hit the ceiling: P 146

(to) hit the nail on the head: D 28, D 30, D 87

(to) hold in check: T 29

(to) hold in low esteem: T 42

holiday: D 303

home: A 10

home call by a social worker: V 27

honestly: P 14

honest man: H 132

honesty: H 132

honeymoon: L 63

hook and eye: M 1

(to) horrify: D 38

hot-headed: C 25

House of Representatives: C 134

house painter: P 117

How are you?: C 93, Q 32

How awful!: Q 14

How can I have the nerve?: C 123

How can one have the nerve?: C 123

How do you like - - -?: Q 18

How do you say - - -?: C 100

however: A 185, S 105

however much: P 245

How far?: H 106

How goes it?: Q 15

How is it sold?: C 102

How long ago?: C 168

How much?: Q 4
How much does it hold?: C 167
How much do I owe you?: Q 17
How much is it?: A 14, C 102,
    C 162
How much is this?: Q 35
How often?: C 6
How should I know?: Q 30
How unfortunate!: Q 5
human race: G 8
(to) humiliate: P 156
hummingbird: P 13
(to) hurry: D 98
(to) hurry back: V 33
(to) hurt or harm someone: H 81
(to) hurt to the quick: T 104
hydrogen bomb: B 25

I

I am coming: Y 15
I am delighted: Q 8
I became afraid: M 45
I bet (not a real wager): A 119
I bet they are: S 57
I bet you don't!: A 120
iceberg: M 79, T 25
I disagree: N 29
I don't have the least idea: N 76
I don't know: Q 50
I don't like it: M 43, M 49
I don't want to: N 45
if at all: S 87
if even: S 88
if I remember correctly: S 90
if not: D 156, D 325
I forgot to tell you: S 46
if so: E 73
if you would do me the favor: S 91
I give up: D 97, M 44
(to) ignore: H 25
I guess: S 44
I imagine: S 44
ill-behaved: M 3
I loathe it: M 41

impatient: M 5
(to) impede: D 310
I'm pleased to meet you: T 88
important: D 118, D 130
I'm very glad to see you: M 40
I'm very sorry: L 58
in a bad humor: D 161
in about: C 92
in abundance: A 90
in a circle: E 136
in accordance with: C 133, D 104
in accordance with the law: A 188
in addition: D 191
in addition to: A 75, S 131
in advance: C 112, C 129, P 183
inadvertently: S 119
in a jiffy: E 149, E 150, E 153
in a little while: D 276
in all: E 104
in all directions: A 70
in a loud voice: E 159
in a low voice: E 160
in a minute: E 149
in a moment: E 150, E 151
in any case: A 210, D 226
in any event: E 148
in a second: E 150, E 153
in a short while: A 229, D 276,
    D 277
inasmuch as: C 97, C 98
in a way: H 105
in back of: A 303, D 297
in bad faith: D 162
in brief: E 132, E 133
in broad daylight: E 121
in bulk: E 103
in care of: A 199
in case: P 262
in case of (that): E 75
in cold blood: A 132
income tax: I 6
in communication with: A 213
incomplete: A 82
in compliance with: E 77, E 225
in conclusion: E 100

in conflict with: E 255
(to) increase: S 149
(to) incur the hatred of: I 8
in days gone by: E 87
indeed: E 88
in detail: P 220, P 247
indirectly: D 205
indoors: B 3, E 72
in due course: A 135
in duplicate: P 207
in earnest: A 55, D 244
I need it: M 46
in effect: E 157
in either case: E 65
in exchange for: A 7
in fact: D 147, E 88, E 135
in favor of: D 186
(an) infinite quantity: S 107
in force: E 157
(to) inform: D 58, D 70, P 140, P 148
informal: S 101
informal gathering or party: R 34
infrared rays: R 3
in front of: A 212, D 274, F 13
in future: E 62, E 109
in good faith: D 122
in good taste: D 119
in good time: C 129
in half: P 228
in haste: A 44
in honor of: E 116
in jest: D 117, D 126, E 69
inland: T 95
in many respects: E 114
in my opinion: A 86, A 87
in no trouble: A 64
in (at) odd moments: A 126
in one fell swoop: D 236
in one's sleep: E 144
in order: E 131
in order that: A 30, P 33
in other words: E 118, E 183
in particular: E 95
in passing: D 188

in place of: E 111
in plain language: E 70
in plain view: A 57
in poor taste: D 160
in presence of: A 155
in progress: E 85, E 113
in proof of: E 142
in proportion: A 80
in reality: E 135
in relief: D 206
in safety: E 138
insane asylum: C 58
in season: E 139
in shirt sleeves: E 112
in short: A 211, E 100, E 134
inside of: D 275
insignificant: V 6
insincerely: D 135
in small quantities: A 219, D 193
in some way or other: D 230
in (at) spare moments: A 126
in spite of: A 21, A 101
in spite of everything: A 101
in spite of that: A 299, C 130
in spite of the fact that: A 102
instead of: E 111, E 156
in stock: E 98
in substance: E 91
in such a case: E 145
in such a way: D 221
insurance policy: P 136
(to) intend or mean to: P 86, T 60
(to) interfere: H 54
(to) interrupt: C 152
(to) intervene: M 63
in that way: D 140
in the act: E 101
in the background: E 110
in the dark: A 96
in the dead of the night: E 94
in the dead of winter: E 108
in the direction of: C 126
in the distance: A 66, E 110
in the evening: P 229
in the event of: E 74

in the final analysis: A 29
in the future: D 106, E 107
in the hands of: E 123
in the latest fashion: A 49
in the long run: A 48
in the manner of: A 37, A 134
in the middle: P 228
in the morning, etc.: P 227
in the nick of time: E 92
in the night air: A 237
in the open: A 8
in the open air: A 190, A 233
in the opposite way: A 236
in the same way: D 270
in the style of: A 72
in this vicinity: P 189
in this way: D 142
in this world: D 224
in those days: E 66
in time: A 137
in token of: E 142
in transit: D 188, D 227
in truth: A 55, D 244
in turn: E 136
in vain: E 67
In view of: E 158
in vogue: D 170
in writing: P 318
ironing board: T 1
irrelevant: F 20, I 7
I should say not!: D 175
I should say so!: Y 9
Is that so?: D 244, D 245, N 24
It can't be helped: N 38, N 79
It disgusts me: M 41
It does not concern me: N 26
It doesn't matter: N 42, N 77
It grieves me: M 42
I think: S 44
It ignores: H 14
It is all over: H 2, H 3, S 42,
    Y 13
It is all right: E 217
It is a long time since I played, etc.:
    H 17

It is better: M 34
It is clear: Y 14
It is cloudy: E 203
It is cold: H 16
It is cool: H 15
It is dusty: H 119
It is foggy (or misty): H 118
It is forbidden: S 47
It is good (bad) weather: H 12
It is hopeless: N 79
It is hot: H 13
It is moonlight: H 116
It is muddy. H 115
It is necessary to: H 120
It is not worth the trouble: V 2
It is no wonder that: N 27
It is obvious: S 40
It is obvious that: S 50
It is rumored that: S 49
It is said: S 41
It is storming: H 122, H 123
It is sunny: H 19, H 121
It is time for: E 184
It is time to go: E 184
It is trying (about) to rain: Q 53
It is unnecessary (superfluous):
    E 203
It is windy: H 10, H 20, H 124
It is yet to be done: E 304
It makes me sick: M 41
It makes no difference: D 89,
    E 185, L 54, N 42
It may be that: P 299, T 9
It must: D 211
It must be: D 252
It must be true: H 1
It probably is: D 252
It's a deal: T 156
It's almost time: F 5
It seems to be impossible: P 45
It seems to me that: M 48
It serves me right: B 10
It's none of your (my, etc.)
    business: N 25
It's not important: N 77

It's not opportune: N 85
It's not to the point: N 85
It's not worthwhile: N 81
It's time to - - -: Y 5
It's too late now: Y 6
It's true: E 182
It tastes good: S 1
It won't be long now: Y 7
I would rather not: P 279

J

jack of all trades: A 283
jet airplane: A 310
jet engine: M 83
jet propulsion: P 296
(to) jilt: D 13
(to) join (a club, etc.): I 11
joint account: C 174
jokingly: D 117
(to) judge: T 72
judgment day: D 302
juggler: J 6
(to) jump: D 78
(to) jump at conclusions: H 33
just: N 5
just about to: Y 8
just as: A 291, S 54
just as is: A 295
just in case: P 242, P 262
just plain: A 295
just right: A 196, A 227
just yesterday: A 312

K

(to) keep: Q 43
(to) keep accounts: LL 14
(to) keep good time (a watch):
   A 265
(to) keep in bounds: T 29
(to) keep one's feet: T 87
(to) keep one's word: C 182
Keep out!: P 294

(to) keep silent: G 15
(to) keep track of: LL 17
(to) keep up-to-date: T 30
(to) kick out: D 20
(to) kill two birds with one stone:
   M 36
kitchen utensils: T 150
(to) kneel: P 174
(to) kneel down: H 129
knitted: D 200
(to) knit the eyebrows: F 16
(to) knock down: E 22
(to) know absolutely nothing
   (about that): N 56
(to) know by heart: S 4
(to) know by sight: C 135
(to) know how to: S 2
knowingly: A 130

L

(to) lack: H 40
lack of instructions: F 2, F 3
(a) lame excuse: D 318
(to) land: S 31, T 137
landing field: C 42
landing gear: T 158
landing strip: P 121
(a) large number of: U 13
last month: E 39
(the) last straw: L 4
last week: L 13
last year: E 39
late: A 31
later on: M 22
(the) latter: E 49
(to) laugh at: R 19
(to) laugh off: T 126
(to) laugh up one's sleeve: R 20
launching pad: P 128
law-abiding: O 4
lawnmower: C 151
(to) leap: D 78
leap year: A 278
(to) learn by heart: A 282

(the) least of it: L 50
(to) leave: S 23
(to) leave alone: D 264, D 266
(to) leave word: D 263
ledger: L 43
leisure hours: R 5
(to) lend: D 66
lengthwise: A 65
less and less: C 9
less than: M 58
(to) let be: D 264
Let him (or them) - - - - -: Q 1
(to) let loose: S 139
Let me out: D 269
(to) let on: D 265
(to) let oneself be coaxed: H 88
Let's see if: A 154
letter of credit: L 28
license plate: P 122
life boat: B 26, L 19
life imprisonment: P 290
life insurance: S 56, S 59
(to) lift with the wrist or hand: L 33
light-hearted: L 45
like: A 37, A 72, P 46
like always: C 106
limestone: P 110
linen: R 43
lipstick: L 20
literally: A 228
little by little: P 132
little finger: D 257
little more: Y 2
Little pitchers have big ears: H 117
(to) live by stealing: V 29
(to) live together: H 80
(to) loan on credit: D 5
(to) lock the door: E 15
long ago: H 18
(a) long time: L 23
look: P 309
(to) look out the corner of one's
    eye: M 71
(to) look towards: D 3
(to) look well: T 34

(to) lose face: P 97
(to) lose one's head: S 32
(to) lose one's mind: P 92, P 95
(to) lose patience: S 32
(to) lose sight of: P 91
(to) lose time: P 93
loss of consciousness: E 161
(a) lot of: A 74
(a) lot of people: P 276
lots of: A 74
loud voice: E 159
love affair: A 309
low-class people: G 9
lower case letter: L 31
low gear: P 288
lumber yard: D 279
lump in the throat: U 7

M

madly: C 113
magic wand: V 8
(to) mail (a letter): E 4, E 30
mail delivery: R 25
mail train: T 157
(the) main floor (usually 2nd):
    P 120
mainland: T 97
mainspring (of a watch): M 88
(the) majority of: L 6, L 7
(the) majority of the people: E 42
(to) make a clean copy: P 153
(to) make a deal: H 74
(to) make a dent: H 55
(to) make a fool of: P 156
(to) make a good showing: H 23
(to) make a mistake: N 20
(to) make an appointment: D 81
(to) make a poor showing: H 53
(to) make a ridiculous blunder:
    H 78
(to) make arrangements: H 22
(to) make eyes at: H 26
(to) make faces: H 57
(to) make faces at: H 45

(to) make friends with: H 86
(to) make fun of: B 38, H 29, H 30
(to) make good: T 33
(to) make hay while the sun
    shines: H 70
(to) make known: D 4
(to) make laugh: H 46
(to) make no difference: D 52,
    N 41
(to) make oneself understood:
    H 93
(to) make one's living: G 6
(to) make trouble: D 36
(to) make up after a quarrel: H 51
(to) make up for: R 31
(to) make use of: V 5
(to) make way for: A 160
man and wife: M 18
manned space ship: N 9
man of worth: H 135
Many happy returns: M 84
Many thanks: M 85
many times: S 128
many ups and downs: M 86
many years: L 23
(to) map: L 38
(to) marry (someone): C 62
master key: LL 7
masterpiece: O 3
(to) match: H 47
mature: H 126
maybe: A 68, T 8
May he (they or you) be (or do)
    - - - - -: Q 1
May I help you?: P 300
meadowlark: A 253
(to) mean: Q 49
meantime: A 268
(a) mean trick: U 14
meanwhile: E 178, M 67
(to) measure: T 139
mechanics shop: T 10
(to) meddle: M 63
mediocre person: M 51
(to) meet: C 159, E 165, T 166

(to) meet face-to-face: E 167
menu: L 48
merry-go-round: T 98
middle finger: D 255
Mind your own business: Q 51
mink wrap: E 286
minor person: M 57
mint (re money): C 59
minutes of a meeting: P 291
(to) misconstrue: T 129
(to) misinterpret: T 129
(to) miss: E 7
(to) miss the train: P 94
moment to moment: P 226
money order: G 10
mongrel dog: P 99
monkey wrench: LL 6
more or less: A 255
moreover: P 234
more than: M 28, M 31
more than anyone: M 32
more than enough: D 216
more than ever: M 33
more than once: M 29, U 18
most of: L 6, L 7
(to) mourn: E 226
movable possessions: B 15
(to) move (residence): M 87
much goings up and down: M 86
(a) "must": D 211
My eyes water: M 47
My mouth waters: S 45
my own car: M 65
my own house: M 65

N

naked: E 83
namely: A 129
naturalization papers: C 54
naturally: C 77, D 222
navy: M 19
near at hand: A 216
near to: C 69, J 9

O

odd number: N 93
of about: D 240
of age: M 39
Of course: C 77, C 96, D 289,
    P 266, S 58, Y 14
Of course not: C 78
of excellent quality: D 166
official identification card: C 66
off stage: E 174
of good quality: D 124
of good stock: D 121
of last month: D 272
of little value or importance:
    D 192, L 50
of one piece: D 235
often: A 84
of that kind: P 211
of the same sort: D 270
oil field: Y 16
oil painting: P 118
(to) O.K.: D 25
old-fashioned: A 40
(to) omit: P 59
on: E 163
on account of: A 11, C 119, P 250
on a large scale: E 102
on all fours: A 36
on all sides: P 39
on an average: P 267
on approval: A 156
on behalf of: D 186, E 125
on board: A 1
once again: D 177
once and for all: D 237, D 238
once in a blue moon: A 257,
    C 110, D 223
once in a while: U 17
Once upon a time: H 4
on credit: A 18, A 105, A 207
on doing something: A 189
one at a time: D 239, U 20
one by one: U 21
on edge: D 129
one must: H 120
on end: D 198

one of these fine days: U 2
one or the other: E 57
one way: D 233
one week from today: D 150
(the) one who (or which): E 53
(the) one with: E 44
on foot: A 103
on hand: E 98
onion skin: T 22
on installments: E 60
only: N 5, N 43
only yesterday: A 312
on one's back: D 141
on one's knees: D 212
on purpose: D 197
on returning: A 59
on sale: D 243
on the bias: A 238, A 239
on the contrary: A 198, P 209
on the dot: E 127
on the fence: E 173
on the following day: A 206,
    A 222
on the inside: P 201
on the lookout for: E 210
on the occasion of: C 119
on the other hand: E 71, P 254,
    P 255
on the other side of: A 223
on the outside: P 224
on the rebound: D 205
on the road to: C 37
on the run: A 44
on the sly: A 24, A 38
on the spur of the moment: D 125
on the way: D 128, D 227, E 246
on the way to: C 37
on the way up: D 219
on time: A 2, A 137
on tiptoes: D 199
on top of: P 213
on vacation: D 242
on watch: E 154
open door: P 305
openly: A 63, A 203, S 115

P

play on words: J 2
(to) play second fiddle: S 76
pleasant time: B 32
please: H 36, H 103, P 221
(to) please: C 10, C 14, D 37
Please be quiet: C 30
Please do it: S 123
Please say it again: R 29
(The) pleasure is mine: E 48
(to) pledge: E 58
point blank: A 122
point of land: L 27
polar bear: O 15
police inspection of a house:
     V 27
(to) polish (shoes): D 35, D 55
poor artist: P 117
poor memory: M 56
porcupine: P 303
porthole: O 10
(to) pose as: D 103
(to) possess scant knowledge:
     E 253
(to) post: E 4
postal money order: G 10
postcard: T 20
(to) postpone: D 49
potable water: A 175
power: F 22
(to) praise: P 150
(to) praise to the skies: P 164
pregnant: E 97
prerequisite: R 30
presence of mind: P 285
Present!: A 136
(to) pretend: D 6, D 265, H 64
(to) pretend not to hear: H 91
(to) pretend not to notice: H 90
(to) pretend to be dead: H 96
(to) prick up one's ears: A 183
pride: A 262
print: L 32
printed letters: L 32
printing error: E 180
private lessons: L 26

private soldier: S 136
pro and con: E 52
prominent: D 206
(to) promise: E 58
prone: B 20
- - -proof: A 113
proud: D 130
provided: S 98
provided that: C 128, D 2, S 97
(a) prudent man: H 137
publicly: A 63
(to) publish: D 7, S 6
(to) pull: T 100
(to) pull over to the right:
     D 296, H 84
pumice: P 111
pun: J 2
(to) pursue: D 14
push button: B 27
(to) put into practice: P 165
(to) put in writing: H 61
(to) put on airs: D 95, D 99, S 150
(to) put oneself in a ridiculous
     situation: T 102
(to) put one's foot in one's
     mouth: M 61
(to) put on weight: E 6, G 4
(to) put the cart before the horse:
     T 129

Q

(to) quarrel with: M 62
(to) question: P 149
question mark: S 99
(to) queue up: H 27
quickly: A 242, D 195, D 232,
     E 152

R

rabble: G 9
(to) rack one's brain: D 298,
     Q 37, R 42

rainbow: A 287
(to) rain cats and dogs: LL 23
rain or shine: Q 22
(to) raise a rumpus: D 12
rapidly: A 23
rate of exchange: T 99
rather: M 26, M 55
rather late: A 247
rather than: A 275, M 27
(to) rattle off: R 27
razor: N 7
(to) reach: P 176
ready cash: D 313
real estate: B 14, B 16
(to) realize (that): C 13, D 93
really: D 244, E 88, E 155
(the) real truth: L 9
reception room: S 16
(to) reckon with: C 139
(to) re-copy: P 153
record: P 291
recording head: C 4
reduced price: D 178
(to) reflect on: P 43
(to) refuse to answer: N 11
(to) regain consciousness: V 34
regardless of: S 108
regards to: R 12
(to) regret: P 100
(to) regret very much: S 63
regular soldier: S 135
reinforced concrete: C 67
(to) reject: D 13
reliable: D 312
reluctantly: D 159
(to) rely on: C 132, C 139
(to) remember or recollect: H 56
remorse: G 17
(to) render first aid: H 82
repeatedly: S 128
(to) repeat mechanically: R 27
(to) reproach: D 27, E 9
(to) resemble: S 19
(to) resist stubbornly: H 89, P 175
(the) rest of them: L 60

(to) restrain: T 101
retail: P 247
(to) return for: V 36
(to) review: P 61
rewind reel: B 19
(to) ride bareback: M 81
(to) ride horseback: I 12
right away: E 89
right here: A 286
right now: A 187, E 141, M 23
right on the face: E 122
right side out: A 201
ripe: E 139
(to) rise: P 180
(to) risk: C 148, P 142
rocket propulsion: P 297
roller coaster: M 80
roller skates: P 73
room and board: P 87
round about: A 52
round-trip ticket: B 17, I 1
rubber band: L 44
(to) ruin: D 8, D 9, E 3
rumor: D 180
(to) run away: E 1

S

saddle: S 100
safe: A 131
(a) safe (strong box): C 19
safe against - - -: A 113
safe and sound: S 36
safe deposit box (in a bank): C 18
safety belt: C 75
safety pin: A 244
sailboat: B 37
salt water: A 171, A 176
(the) same as: E 51, I 3
sandpaper: P 25
satchel: S 13
(to) satisfy a need or desire: M 37
(to) save one's skin: S 34
(to) save time: G 5

string of pearls: H 128
strong box: C 19
(to) study hard: Q 48
(to) stumble: D 79, D 100
stylish: D 119, D 170
(to) succeed: T 33
such a big mistake: T 11
such as: T 5, T 6
such as that: P 211
suddenly: D 144, D 196,
    D 208, D 220
suds: E 200
sugar plantation or refinery: I 10
(to) suit: V 15
suitable: A 112
(to) suit perfectly: V 13
summing up: E 133
(to) sum up: E 76
(to) sunbathe: T 130
sun dial: R 22
sun glasses: G 1
sunrise: S 18
sunrise to sunset: D 217
sunset: P 311
superfluous: E 202
supine: B 21, D 141
supposing: D 1, S 155
sure enough: D 308
(to) surprise: P 81
(to) survey: L 38
suspension bridge: P 301
(a) swarm of people: U 5
(to) swear: E 27
(to) sweat blood: S 152
(to) sweat profusely: S 152
sweet-tempered: C 109
swell of the sea: M 16
swiftly: A 128
swiftness of time: C 150
(to) swindle: D 34

T

tail light: F 7, F 8
tail pipe: T 168

(to) take: Q 43
(to) take a chance: C 148
(to) take a drink: E 28
(to) take advantage of the situation:
    A 284
(to) take after (someone): S 19
(to) take a jump: P 82
(to) take a long time in doing
    something: T 17
(to) take a long weekend: H 65
(to) take an afternoon nap:
    D 329
(to) take a nap: D 283, E 26,
    E 31
(to) take an auto ride: P 69
(to) take a picture: S 12
(to) take as a joke: T 124
(to) take a stand against: S 21
(to) take a step: D 75, T 139
(to) take a stroll: D 86
(to) take a walk: P 66
(to) take a walk or ride: D 73
(to) take care: T 41
(to) take care of: P 283
(to) take care of someone: M 72
(to) take charge (of): E 162, H 87
(to) take dictation: E 188
(to) take exercise: H 35
(to) take for a - - -: T 72
(to) take for granted: D 61, D 62,
    D 63, D 64, D 65
(to) take into account: H 24, T 44,
    T 131
(to) take it (I'll take it): Q 43
(to) take it easy: T 140
(to) take lightly: T 126
(to) take pity on: T 64
(to) take place: T 65
(to) take root: E 23
(to) take the lead: T 133
(to) take time off: T 136
(to) take to heart: T 125, T 132
(to) take to one's heels: P 162
(to) take undue liberties: P 54
take-up reel: B 19, C 52

(the) talk of the town: L 1
(to) talk too much: H 9
(to) talk to oneself: H 8
(to) taste like: S 3
(to) teach a course: E 291, R 18
(to) tear into strips: H 66
(to) tear to pieces: H 44, H 72
(to) tease: D 16, T 128
tea set: J 3
teddy bear: O 19
telephone book (directory): G 16
telephone receiver: R 9
tenement: C 61
test tube: T 167
(to) thank, or give thanks: D 50
That can't be helped: E 195
that depends: S 54
that is: A 129
That is a horse of a different color:
    E 193
That is even worse: P 89
That is it: E 191
That is the limit!: E 192
That is to say: E 183, O 1
That is urgent: E 190
That is why: P 186, P 217
that long: A 292
That's enough!: Q 7
That's not the point: N 61
That's not the question: N 61
That's right: E 191
That's the last straw: N 30
That's the least of the trouble:
    E 185
That's the point: A 184
That was true: E 196
that way: P 187
that which: L 55
theatre stub for re-entry: C 143
The coast is not clear: H 117
The fact is: E 41
the more - - - the less: M 66
then: A 53
the ones: L 61
the one who (the one which): E 53

the one with: E 44
The pleasure is mine: E 48
thereafter: D 294
There are no two ways about it:
    N 36
therefore: A 296, A 297, P 197,
    P 198, P 215, P 219, P 233,
    P 243
There is more than meets the eye:
    H 114
There is no doubt: N 18
There is no hope: N 39
There is no way around it: N 36,
    N 39
There is no way out of it: N 39
There is the difficulty!: A 259
There's no hurry: N 35
There's no need to: N 34
There's no other way but to - - -:
    N 33
There's nothing to do except: N 33
There's no two ways about it: N 80
the same as: A 291, E 51
The thing did not jell (work well):
    L 2
The time limit expired. S 51
they say: S 41
thief: L 21
(to) think about: P 86
(to) think not: C 157
(to) think so: C 158
this side of: M 21
this way: P 181, P 188
This will do: A 294
thoroughbred horse: C 1
thoroughly: A 34
those which: L 61
those who: L 61
(A) thousand thanks: M 68
throng: R 24
through (throughout): A147,
    A 241, D 185, P 196, P 206
through thick and thin: P 269
through train: T 161, T 164
(to) throw a party: D 82

(to) throw a stone: M 8
(to) throw bouquets: E 11
thumb: D 258
(to) tighten the reins: T 101
tilted: D 154
tin foil: H 130, P 22
(to) tip: D 67
(to) tip one's hat: T 108
tire tread: R 38
tissue paper: P 28
to and fro: D 113
to boot: D 191
toe: D 256
together: A 56
toilet paper: P 30
toll call: LL 1
tomorrow afternoon: M 12
Tomorrow is another day: M 9
tomorrow morning: M 10
tomorrow night: M 11
to myself: P 32
tonight: A 50
Too bad!: Q 16
to oneself: C 136
toothache: D 324
toothbrush: C 68
toothpick: P 16
tooth powder: P 137
top hat: S 140
to right and left: P 39
to the hair: A 196
to the left: A 47
to the limit (or utmost): H 107
to the point: A 133, D 189
to the right: A 45
to the utmost: A 76, D 157,
     H 107
(to) touch a very sensitive spot:
     T 104
towards: A 111
towards the end of (a period
     of time): A 31
(to) track down: D 14
trademark: M 17
trade union: G 13

traffic jam: A 168
(The) train was x minutes late:
     E 55
travel bureau: O 6
traveler's check: CH 1
traveling salesman: A 167
treacherously: A 146
(to) treat of: T 153
trim: B 12
(to) trip: D 79, D 100
trousseau: E 179, G 2
truly, truthfully: D 245, E 155
(to) trust: C 132
trustworthy: D 312
(to) try to: T 153, V 20
(to) tune up a motor: P 141
(to) turn (around): D 48
(to) turn a deaf ear: H 91
(to) turn down the radio: B 2
(to) turn down the volume:
     D 319
(to) turn on (light, radio, etc.):
     P 158
(to) turn one's back (on):
     D 41, V 30
(to) turn out to be: V 12, V 14
(to) turn the corner: D 320
(to) turn the page: D 90
(to) turn to the right: T 134
(to) turn up (or down) a radio,
     etc.: P 161
two by two: D 138
two-faced: D 137
two of a kind: T 7
two-way: D 139
two weeks (from today): D 151,
     Q 54
(to) typewrite: E 187
typewriter: M 13
typewritten: E 189
typing error: E 181

U

unanimously: A 151

unavoidable: S 117
unbound: E 137
uncovered: E 86
undecided: E 173
under: D 251
underclothes: P 19
underclothing: R 44
under cover: A 24
under full sail: A 141
under no circumstances: P 253
under observation: E 117
under penalty of: S 126
under pretext (or pretense) of:
　　S 127
underside: L 17
(to) understand: T 49
(to) undertake: P 165
under the guise of: S 124
under the pretext of: S 125, S 127
unequalled: S 109
uneven number: N 93
unexpectedly: A 20, A 68, D 125,
　　D 152, E 45
unfortunately: P 202
unharmed: A 131
unless: A 83, A 92, C 95
unlucky: D 164
unnecessary: D 216
unnoticed: S 110
unpaid: E 86
unreserved: S 118
until: H 112
until full: H 113
unusual: F 19
unwillingly: A 41, D 159, D 163,
　　S 114
uphill: C 179
upon: E 163
upon my honor: S 130
upright piano: P 106
ups and downs: S 147
upside down: P 72
upstream: A 179, C 140, R 37
up the street: C 28
up to a point: H 105

up-to-date: A 49, H 109
up to now: H 104, H 109
up to the top: H 108
usual: D 181
usually: P 235, P 240, P 260

V

(to) vanish: P 98
vanity: A 262
various times: R 26
vertical: A 106
very bad luck: S 153
very close: A 122
very early in the morning:
　　M 93
very far away: E 93
(the) very man: E 50
very much: C 115, D 157
very often: C 120, M 92
very soon: P 135, Y 8
(the) very thought of: L 8
violently: A 128
(to) visé (visa) a passport:
　　R 16
visibly: A 95
(to) vouch for: D 32, S 25

W

waiting room: S 14
(to) wait table: S 85
(to) wait the whole blessed day:
　　E 199
(to) walk: I 14
(to) walk by: D 83
(to) walk the streets: M 54
want ads: A 311
wanted: S 48
(to) want to: T 42
warship: N 10
war supplies: M 89
(to) wash one's hands: L 25
waste paper: P 21

(to) watch out for: T 41
waterfall: S 33
water ski: E 201
wax paper: P 29
(his) weakness (or weakside):
    L 18, S 145
(to) wear: LL 18, T 144
We are even (quits): E 206, N 46
(to) wear oneself out: H 100
(to) weather the storm: A 177
week before last: L 11
weekday: D 301, D 304
weekdays: D 307
weekend: E 47
(to) welcome: D 40
well (well - - - look): P 309
well and good: S 37
Well done!: A 298
well-done (well-cooked): B 8, B 9
well-groomed: B 12
well now - - -: A 185
well then: P 308
well worth it: D 311
wetback: P 18
What a beauty!: Q 6
What a lot!: Q 4
What a mess!: Q 3
What an atrocity!: Q 2
What a pity!: Q 16
What a pleasure!: Q 8
What a tongue-twister!: Q 25
What can I do for you?: E 128,
    Q 30
What can I serve you?: Q 30
What can I show you?: Q 30
What does it deal with?: D 202
What does it mean?: Q 28, Q 32
What do you mean?: Q 29
What do you think of it?: Q 18
What for?: P 34
What happened?: Q 27
what has been said: L 51
What if - - -?: Y 4
What is it?: Q 9
What is it about:? D 202

What is it good for?: P 37
what is more: M 25
What is it used for?: P 35, P 36
What is the date?: A 19
What is the point of that?: A 121
What is the use of it?: Q 36
What is your name?: C 101
What nonsense!: Q 2
What's eating you?: Q 24
What's it to you?: Q 51
What size is it?: D 203
What's going on?: Q 26
What's new?: Q 12
What's so bad about that?: Q 11
What's that to me?: A 89
What's the difference?: Q 23
What's the matter?: Q 9, Q 10
What's the matter with you?: Q 19
What's up?: Q 15, Q 26
What's wrong with it?: Q 34
What's wrong with that?: Q 11
What time is it?: Q 13
What would you like to buy?:
    Q 30
whenever: C 165, S 97, T 110
when least expected: E 45
where: P 206
Where are you going?: A 165
whereas: V 28
wherever: A 166, D 326
whether one likes it or not: P 230
whether you wish or not: Q 52
which: P 206
which caused: L 56
Which is which?: C 161
Which way?: P 206
while: E 146
(to) while away the time: P 56
(to) whisper: H 7
whispering: E 160
white of an egg: C 76
whitewash: Y 18
Who is calling?: D 187
Who knows?: Q 50
(the) whole truth: L 15

Y

Z

SECTION III

SOME COLORFUL SPANISH EXPRESSIONS
WITH THE LITERAL AND FREE
TRANSLATIONS TO ENGLISH "SIDE-BY-SIDE"

Notes: Sometimes a colorful idiomatic expression in one language loses much of its color (idiomatic appeal) when translated to another language. Not all, but most of the expressions of this section are interesting and colorful in both Spanish and English.

Some of the literal translations in this section can be approximations only.

SPAN.: A buen hambre no hay pan duro.
LIT.:   For good hunger there is no hard bread.
FREE: Anything tastes good when you're hungry.

SPAN.: A donde fueres haz lo que vieres.
LIT: Wherever you go, do what (as) you see (being done).
FREE: When in Rome do as the Romans do.

SPAN.: A otro perro con ese hueso
LIT.:   To another dog with that bone
FREE: You're putting me on.

SPAN.: Ahora que hay modo
LIT.:   Now that there is a way or mood
FREE: Make the most of the opportunity.
             Make hay while the sun shines.

SPAN.: Al hierro caliente batir de repente.
LIT.:   Beat the hot iron at once.
FREE: Strike while the iron is hot.

SPAN.: Antes que te cases mira lo que haces.
LIT.:   Before you marry look what you do.
FREE: Look before you leap.

SPAN.: "Aramos," dijo la mosca al buey.
LIT.:   "Let's plough," said the fly to the ox.
SPAN.: "Vamos arando," decía un mosquito al buey.
LIT.:   "Let's get plowing," said the mosquito to the ox.
FREE: "What a dust I've raised," said the fly upon the coach.

SPAN.: Beben agua en el mismo jarrito.
LIT.: They drink water from the same little jug.
FREE: Thick as thieves; hand in glove

SPAN.: Cada perico a su estaca, cada changa a su mecate
LIT.: Each parakeet (or parrot) on his perch, each monkey on his rope
FREE: To each his own.

SPAN.: Cada quien tiene su modo de dar chiche.
LIT.: Each has her way of giving the breast (to nurse).
SPAN.: Cada quien tiene su manera de matar pulgas.
LIT.: Each person has his way to kill fleas.
FREE: There's more than one way to skin (kill) a cat.
       You don't have to choke a cat to death on butter.

SPAN.: Caras vemos, corazones no sabemos.
LIT.: Faces we see, hearts we don't know.
FREE: You can't tell a book by its cover.

SPAN.: Claro como el agua de Xochimilco
LIT.: Clear as the water of Xochimilco
FREE: Clear as mud

SPAN.: Comer frijoles y repetir pollo
LIT.: To eat beans and belch chicken
SPAN.: Comer frijoles y eructar jamón
LIT.: To eat beans and belch ham
FREE: Weak to perform though mighty to pretend

SPAN.: Como el burro que tocó la flauta
LIT.: Like the burro that played the flute
FREE: By a stroke of luck; by pure chance

SPAN.: Como quitarle un pelo a un gato
LIT.: Like the losing (dropping, falling, shedding) of a hair of a cat
FREE: Like a drop in the bucket

SPAN.: Con estos bueyes hay que arar.
LIT.: With these burros one must plow.
FREE: One must make do with what one has.

SPAN.: **Contigo la milpa es rancho y el atole es champurado.**
LIT.: With you the cornfield is an estate and the corn-meal drink is "champagne."
FREE: Love in a cottage

SPAN.: **Cual el cuervo, tal su huevo**
LIT.: Which (such) raven (crow or buzzard), such an egg
SPAN.: **Cuando el tronco sale bueno, las astillas son de ley.**
LIT.: When the trunk comes out (does) well the chips are of the law (regular, of good quality).
SPAN.: **De tal jarro, tal tepalcate**
LIT.: Of such a jug, such a potsherd (jug fragment)
SPAN.: **De tal palo, tal astilla**
LIT.: From such a pole (tree) such chips
SPAN.: **De tal padre, tal hijo**
LIT.: From such a father, such a son
SPAN.: **El hijo de la gata, ratones mata.**
LIT.: The son of the cat kills mice.
FREE: Like father, like son; chip off the old block

SPAN.: **Cuando las víboras andaban paradas**
LIT.: When snakes walked upright
FREE: In olden times, way back when, long ago

SPAN.: **Dar la suave (a uno)**
LIT.: To give the smooth (or soft) to someone
FREE: To sweet talk someone; to butter-up or soft-soap someone
To polish the apple

SPAN.: **Darle un beso a la botella**
LIT.: To give the bottle a kiss
FREE: To take a nip or swig

SPAN.: **De la subida más alta es la caída más lastimosa**
LIT.: Of the highest rise the sorriest fall
FREE: Pride goeth before a fall.
The bigger they are the harder they fall.

SPAN.: **Desnudar un santo para vestir otro**
LIT.: To strip one saint bare to clothe another
FREE: To rob Peter to pay Paul

SPAN.: Después de atole
LIT.:   After the atole (corn meal drink)

FREE: Hindsight is better than foresight.

SPAN.: Donde las espaldas pierden su nombre
LIT.:   Where the back loses its name

FREE: The "lower part of the back" where you sit
        The topmost part of the legs
        The back of the lap

SPAN.: ¿Dónde quedó la bolita?
LIT: Where did the little ball stay?

FREE: Hocus-pocus, sleight of hand

SPAN.: El agua es para los bueyes, el vino para los hombres.
LIT.:   Water is for oxen, wine is for men.

FREE: Let the fish drink water.

SPAN.: El campo fértil no descansado, tórnase estéril.
LIT.:   The unrested fertile field turns sterile.

FREE: All work and no play makes Jack a dull boy.

SPAN.: El miedo no anda en burro.
LIT.:   Fear does not go (ride) on a burro.

FREE: Fear hath wings; fear lends one wings.

SPAN.: El perico dice lo que sabe, pero no sabe lo que dice.
LIT.:   The parrot says what he knows, but doesn't know what he says.

FREE: To say something by rote

SPAN.: En caliente y de repente
LIT.:   In heat and suddenly

FREE: Strike while the iron is hot.

SPAN.: En casa del herrero, cuchillo de palo
LIT.:   In the blacksmith's house, a wooden knife

FREE: The blacksmith's mare and the shoemaker's children are the worst shod.

SPAN.: En menos que canta un gallo
LIT.:   In less (time) than the rooster sings (crows)

FREE: In no time at all; quick as a wink; in the shake of a lamb's tail

SPAN.: ¿En qué cama hemos dormido juntos?
LIT.:   In what bed have we slept together?
FREE: Do I know you? How did we get so friendly?

SPAN.: Entrada de caballo y salida de burro
LIT.:   Entrance on horseback, exit on a burro
FREE: Don't start something you can't finish.

SPAN.: Es burro que no rebuzna porque olvidó la tonada.
LIT.:   He is a burro that doesn't bray because he forgot the tune.
FREE: Not to know enough to come in out of the rain

SPAN.: Es como llevar piedras al cerro.
LIT.:   It is like carrying stones to the hill.
FREE: Like carrying coals to Newcastle

SPAN.: Eso es harina de otro costal (E 193 of SEC. I).
LIT.:   That is flour from another (different) sack.
FREE: That is a horse of another color.
        That's a different story or situation.

SPAN.: Estar como agua para chocolate.
LIT.:   It is like water for chocolate.
FREE: To be beside oneself, burned up, mad as a hornet, etc.

SPAN.: Estar como perro en barrio ajeno
LIT.:   To be like a dog in the neighbor's yard
FREE: To feel out of place
        To feel like a fish out of water
        To feel like a square peg in a round hole

SPAN.: Estar entre la espada y la pared (E 263 of SEC. I)
LIT.:   To be between the sword and the wall
FREE: To be between the devil and the deep blue sea

SPAN.: Estar podrido en dinero
LIT.:   To be rotten with money
SPAN.: Tener más lana que un borrego
LIT.:   To have more wool than a lamb
FREE: To be on easy street; to have money to burn

SPAN.: **Falta lo mero bueno.**
LIT.: The true (real) good is lacking.
FREE: We are not out of the woods yet; it's not over yet.

SPAN.: **Gato escaldado del agua fría huye.**
LIT.: The scalded cat flees (even) cold water.
FREE: A burnt child dreads the fire.

SPAN.: **Hacer lo que otro no puede hacer por uno**
LIT.: To do what no other can do for one
SPAN.: **Ir a donde el rey va solo**
LIT.: To go where the king goes alone
FREE: To go to the washroom
To go to powder one's nose

SPAN.: **Hacer patitos en el agua**
LIT.: To make little ducklings on the water
FREE: To skim or skip stones on top of the water

SPAN.: **Hacerse de la boca chiquita**
LIT.: To make a tiny little mouth
FREE: To be prissy, fussy

SPAN.: **La carne de burro no es transparente.**
LIT.: The flesh of the burro is not transparent.
FREE: I can't see through you.

SPAN.: **Le patina el coco.**
LIT.: His coconut (head) slips.
FREE: To be crazy; to have a screw loose

SPAN.: **Más larga que la cuaresma**
LIT.: Longer than Lent
FREE: Never ending

SPAN.: **Más loco que una cabra**
LIT.: Crazier than a goat
FREE: As mad as a hatter; fit to be tied

SPAN.: **Más vale llegar a tiempo que en convidado**
LIT.: Better to arrive on time (early) than to be invited
FREE: First come, first served

SPAN.: Más vale pájaro en mano que ciento volando.
LIT.:   A bird in the hand is worth more than 100 flying.
....
FREE: A bird in the hand is worth two in the bush.

SPAN.: Meter gato por libre
LIT.:   To put the cat in for free
....
FREE: To take one in; to cheat

SPAN.: Meter la cuchara (or Meter uno su cuchara)
LIT.:   To put the spoon in
....
FREE: To butt in, put one's oar in, put in one's two cents worth

SPAN.: Meterse en Honduras
LIT.:   To put oneself in the depths, to get into Honduras
SPAN.: Meterse entre las patas de los caballos
LIT.:   To put oneself amidst the horses' feet
....
FREE: To get in trouble, go beyond one's depth

SPAN.: Mientras que en mi casa estoy, rey soy.
LIT.:   While in my house, I am king.
....
FREE: A man's house is his castle.

SPAN.: No hay nada tan atrevido como la ignorancia.
LIT.:   There is nothing more bold than ignorance.
....
FREE: Fools rush in where angels fear to tread.

SPAN.: No quiero, no quiero, pero échemelo en el sombrero.
LIT.:   I don't want, I don't want, but throw it in my hat.
....
FREE: Half-heartedly; against one's better judgment

SPAN.: No sabes en que palo te trepas
LIT.:   Not to know which pole (tree) to climb
....
FREE: Not to know what one is up against, or getting into

SPAN.: Otro gallo nos cantará.
LIT.:   Another (different) rooster will sing for us.
....
FREE: That's a different story.
         That's a horse of a different color.

SPAN.: Por sus pistolas
LIT.:   For your pistols
....
FREE: Just because

SPAN.: **Por un pelito de rana**
LIT.: By a little hair of the frog
SPAN.: **Por una nadita**
LIT.: By a little nothing
FREE: It was a close call, a close shave, a near thing.

SPAN.: **Prietitos del mismo arroz**
LIT.: The "little black one's" of the same rice
FREE: It's all in the day's work.
Occupational hazards

SPAN.: **¡Que nombrecito!** (Q 25 of SEC. I)
LIT.: What a cute little name! (Ironic)
FREE: What a tongue-twister!
(Note: The Spanish word **"travalenguas"** also means "tongue-twister".)

SPAN.: **Quedarse como el que chifló en la loma**
LIT.: To remain like the one who whistled on the hill
FREE: To be left holding the bag

SPAN.: **Quedarse con un pie en el estribo**
LIT.: To remain with a foot in the stirrup
FREE: To be left behind

SPAN.: **¿Quién le pone el cascabel al gato?**
LIT.: Who puts the bell on the cat?
FREE: Who will tackle the problem?

SPAN.: **Saberlo de buena fuente**
LIT.: To know it from a good source
FREE: Straight from the horse's mouth

SPAN.: **Sacarse el gordo**
LIT.: To draw the fat one (the big prize of a lottery)
FREE: To hit the jackpot; bring home the bacon

SPAN.: **Salir de Guatemala y meterse en Honduras**
LIT.: To leave Guatemala (bad corn stalks) and put oneself in Honduras
(beyond one's depth; in trouble)
SPAN.: **Salir de Guatemala y meterse en guatepeor**
LIT.: To leave Guatemala (bad corn stalks) and put oneself in "worse
corn stalks"

(continued on next page)

FREE: Out of the frying pan into the fire
         Out of the briars into the thorns

SPAN.: **Ser más vivo que el que asó la manteca**
LIT.:   To be more alive (lively) than he who roasted the fat (backed into the stove?)
SPAN.: **Ser más listo que un coyote**
LIT.:   To be more ready (alert) than a coyote
FREE: Smart as a whip; sharp as a tack; to be a smart guy

SPAN.: **Si esta víbora te pica, no hay remedio en la botica.**
LIT.:   If this snake bites you, there is no remedy at the pharmacy.
FREE: You're playing with fire.

SPAN.: **Si mi tía no hubiera muerto, todavía viviría.**
LIT.:   If my aunt had not died, she would still be alive.
SPAN.: **Si mi tía tuviera ruedas, sería una bicicleta.**
LIT.:   If my aunt had wheels, she would be a bicycle.
FREE: If wishes were horses, beggars would ride.
        If my aunt had been a man, she would have been my uncle.

SPAN.: **Trabajar para el gobierno** (or **trabajar para el inglés**)
LIT.:   To work for the government (or to work for the English)
FREE: To work without pay or profit

SPAN.: **¡Vete a bañar!** (V 24 of SEC. I)
LIT.:   Go take a bath!
SPAN.: **¡Vete a ver si ya puso la cochina** (or **puerca**)!
LIT.:   Go see if the sow has already laid an egg!
SPAN: **¡Vete a echar pulgas a otra parte!**
LIT.:   Go throw (give off) fleas somewhere else (to another party)!
FREE: Go jump in the lake! Go lay an egg!
        Go peddle your papers! Get lost! etc.

SPAN.: **Vivito y coleando**
LIT.:   Alive and wagging tail
FREE: Alive and kicking; bright-eyed and bushy-tailed

SPAN.: **Y colorín, colorado, este cuento se ha acabado.**
LIT.:   And a linnet (pl. = glowing colors), colored (reddish), this story has finished itself.
FREE: And they lived happily ever after.

SPAN.: **Yo pregunto si la manteca es unto.**

LIT.:   I ask if the butter is grease.

FREE: To clear the matter up; to see what is going on

SPAN.: **Yo tengo una tía que toca la guitarra.**

LIT.:   I have an aunt who plays the guitar.

FREE: Let's not change the subject.
        What's that got to do with the price of eggs in China?
        Cider comes from apples.
        So that's new(s)?

SECTION IV

THREE-LETTER NON-COGNATE WORDS
THAT HAVE THE SAME SPELLING
IN SPANISH AND ENGLISH

Spanish meaning (Eng. translation)	Spelling	English meaning
bird	AVE(.)	abr. of "avenue"
lime	CAL(.)	abr. of "California" or "calorie"
dog, trigger of a gun	CAN	a sheet metal container, or to be able
with	CON	to study, against, abr. of "confidence," etc.
gift (knack), title	DON	to put on, to dress
I was or he was	ERA	a period in time
end	FIN	winglike membrane of fish, projecting metallic rib
there is	HAY	grass for fodder
I will go	IRÉ	anger
(you) read (command v. "leer")	LEA	pasture, meadow, a measure of yarn
fight, contest	LID	movable cover, eyelid
sea	MAR	to damage, disfigure
bread	PAN	domestic vessel (usually open and shallow)
pair	PAR	a standard value
foot	PIE	style of pastry, to scramble type
profit, advantage	PRO	for, on behalf of, etc.

net	RED	the hue red
May he (you, etc.) be - - - - -	SEA	ocean or other large body of salt water
without	SIN	violation of divine law, etc.
sun (or musical term)	SOL	musical or chemical term
they are (v. "ser")	SON	male descendant, male child
I am (v. "ser")	SOY	a sauce, a kind of bean
so, as such	TAN	browning of skin by sun, etc.
rhyme, reason	TON	weight of 2000 or 2240 lb. (short or long ton) or 1000 kg. (metric ton)
they go (v. "ir")	VAN	vehicle for moving objects

SECTION V
MISLEADING NON-COGNATES
AND
"PART-TIME" COGNATES

Notes: Some of the following Spanish entries are completely misleading in that the Spanish word suggests an inappropriate English meaning: e.g., **"sopa"** in Spanish does <u>not</u> mean "soap" in English, and **"parientes"** in Spanish does <u>not</u> mean "parents" in English. There are other entries wherein the Spanish word sometimes is suggestive of an English equivalent but has also a very different translation: e.g., **"real"** in Spanish can be interpreted at times to mean "real" in English but more often should be translated as "royal," and **"equipo"** in Spanish can mean "equipment" in English but is more often to be translated as "team."

In the Spanish-to-English column, certain English words are in brackets to indicate that <u>only sometimes</u> the Spanish word has the meaning of the bracketed English word. In the English-to-Spanish column the abbreviations: (a.) = "adjective," (n.) = "noun" and (v.) = "verb," are used in a few cases for clarity.

<u>Spanish-English</u>

ACRE: sharp, sour, rude, harsh, [acre]

ACTUAL: current, present (re time)

ADMIRAR: to amaze, wonder, [admire]

APROVECHAR: to take advantage of

APUNTAR: to point, write down, make a note of

ASIGNACIÓN: allowance, assignment, [assignation]

ASISTIR: to attend, be present, to help, [to assist]

ATENDER: to pay attention, take care of, [attend to]

<u>English-Spanish</u>

ACRE: acre

ACTUAL: verdadero, real

ADMIRE: estimar, admirar

APPROVE: aprobar

APPOINT: nombrar

ASSIGNATION: asignación

ASSIST: ayudar, asistir

ATTEND: asistir a, cuidar, atender

AUTO: sentence, edict, warrant, [automobile]

AUTOMOBILE: coche, carro, auto

CARPETA: letter case, file

CARPET: alfombra

CARTA: letter (re mail), [playing card]

CART: carro, carreta
CARD: tarjeta, naipe, carta

CIGARRO: cigarette

CIGAR: puro

COLEGIO: school (private or high school)

COLLEGE: universidad

CONFERENCIA: lecture, interview, meeting, [conference]

CONFERENCE: junta, sesión, entrevista, conferencia

CONSTIPADO: suffering from a cold

CONSTIPATED: estreñido

CONTAR: to tell, relate, [count]

COUNT: (v.) contar

CONTENTO: happy, glad, satisfied, [contented]

CONTENTED: satisfecho, tranquilo, contento

COSTUMBRE: custom

COSTUME: vestuario

DECEPCIÓN: disillusion, disappointment, [deception]

DECEPTION: engaño, fraude, decepción

DESGRACIA: misfortune, mishap

DISGRACE: (n.) deshonra, vergüenza, estigma

DESGRACIADO: unfortunate, wretched

DISGRACED: deshonrado, degradado

DESHONESTO: immodest, immoral

DISHONEST: engañoso, falso

DIRECCIÓN: address (re mail), [direction]

DIRECTION: dirección

DISGUSTO: quarrel, grief, sorrow, [disgust]

DISGUST: desarón, asco, repugnancia, aversión, disgusto

DISTINTO: different, clear, [distinct]

DISTINCT: claro, visible, diferente, distinto

EMBARAZADA: pregnant

EMBARRASSED: turbado confuso, desconcertado

EQUIPO: team, fittings, [equipment]

EQUIPMENT: aparatos, equipo

EQUIVOCACIÓN: error, mistake

EQUIVOCATION: equívoco subterfugio

ÉXITO: success

EXIT: salida

EXPEDIR: to send, ship, dispatch, [expedite]

EXPEDITE: acelerar, facilitar, meter prisa, expedir

EXPLANAR: to level

EXPLAIN: explicar

FÁBRICA: factory, mill, structure, [fabric]

FABRIC: tela, textura, fábrica

FALTA: shortage, lack, blemish defect, [fault]

FAULT: (n.) culpa (re blame), defecto, faulta

FORMAL: reliable, regular, trustworthy, [formal]

FORMAL: convencional, ceremonioso, formal

FRASE: sentence, [phrase]

PHRASE: expresión, frase

FRAY: priest

FRAY: (v.) raerse, deshilacharse; (n.) reyerta, riña

GOLPE: blow

GULP: (n.) trago

GRACIOSO: amusing, witty

GRACIOUS: afable, cortés

GRANDE: large, [grand]

GRAND: grandioso, magnífico, grande

HONESTO(A): decent, pure, virtuous, chaste

HONEST: honrado, recto

IDIOMA: language

IDIOM: modismo

IGNORAR: to be unaware or ignorant of

IGNORE: no hacer caso de, desatender

LARGO: long

LARGE: grande

LECTURA: reading

LECTURE: (n.) conferencia, discurso

LEER: to read

LEER: (v.) mirar de soslayo, mirar con injuria; (n.) mirada de soslayo

LIAR: to tie, bind, roll up

LIAR: (n.) mentiroso, embustero

MATE: to kill (imperative)	MATE: (n.) compañero, consorte; (v.) aparear(se)
MEDIA: stocking	MEDIA: (pl. of medium) has meanings in science, phonetics, and the news
ORDINARIO: coarse, vulgar, [ordinary]	ORDINARY: corriente, común, ordinario
PROBAR: to test, taste, try out	PROBE: (v.) tentar, reconocer, sondear
QUITAR: to take away, deprive of, subtract	QUIT: abandonar, cesar, parar, dejar (de hacer algo)
RAPÉ: snuff	RAPE: (n.) estupro, violación
REAL: royal, [real]	REAL: (a.) verdadero, real
REALIZAR: to fulfill, achieve, [realize]	REALIZE: darse cuenta de (re comprehend), efectuar (re achieve), realizar
RECORDAR: to remember, recall, remind, awaken	RECORD: (v.) registrar, apuntar, asentar, inscribir
REGULAR: ordinary, so-so, all right, fairly well (re health), [regular]	REGULAR: metódico, ordenado, regular
RENTA: interest, [rent]	RENT: (v.) alquilar; (n.) arrendamiento, renta
REPENTE: start, sudden movement (**de repente** = suddenly)	REPENT: arrepentirse
REPLICAR: to reply, answer, retort, [replicate]	REPLICATE: (v.) duplicar, triplicar, replicar
ROPA: clothes, clothing	ROPE: (n.) soga, cuerda
RUIN: vile, mean, petty, stingy	RUIN: (v.) arruinar, estropear; (n.) ruina
SALVO: safe	SALVO: salva
SANO: healthy, sound, whole, [sane]	SANE: cuerdo, sensato, sano

SAUCE: willow

SAUCE: salsa

SENSIBLE: sensitive, perceptible

SENSIBLE: sensato, razonable, juicioso

SIMPÁTICO: agreeable, pleasant, congenial

SYMPATHETIC: compasivo

SOPA: soup

SOAP: jabón

SUCEDER: to happen, come about, [succeed]

SUCCEED: lograr(se) (+ inf.); medrar, salir bien, suceder

SUCESO: event, incident

SUCCESS: éxito

TALLER[1]: shop, laboratory, studio

TALLER: más alto

TUNA: prickly pear

TUNA: atún

TUTOR: guardian, [tutor]

TUTOR: (n.) maestro particular, tutor

VAGÓN: railway car or coach

WAGON: carro, carreta, carretón

VALE: note, sales slip, coupon

VALE: valle, cañada

VESTIDO: clothing, apparel, suit

VEST: chaleco

---

[1] The American traveler in Mexico frequently sees signs reading "TALLER MECANICO," which means "Mechanics Shop." If a visitor, who has only a slight acquaintance with Spanish, guesses that "TALLER MECANICO" means "taller mechanic," he may be surprised to find a very short man at work inside the shop!

SECTION VI

MASCULINE SPANISH NOUNS WITH ENDINGS USUALLY CONSIDERED FEMININE

Nouns ending in "a" (or "as")

Spanish	English	Spanish	English
abrebotellas	bottle opener	paracaídas	parachute
abrelatas	can opener	paraguas	umbrella
barreminas	minesweeper	patriarca	patriarch
cambiavía	railway switchman	pentagrama	musical staff
cínema	cinema, motion picture	pirata	pirate
		planeta[1]	planet
clima	climate	plasma	plasma
cortaplumas	penknife	poema	poem
crucigrama	crossword puzzle	poeta (f. = poetisa)	poet
cuentagotas	dropper	portamonedas	pocketbook, coin purse
día	day		
diagrama[1]	diagram, graph	portaplumas	penholder
dogma	dogma	problema	problem
drama	drama	profeta	prophet
emblema	emblem	programa	program, plan
enigma	enigma, riddle, puzzle	protoplasma	protoplasm
estigma	stigma, brand, birthmark, mark of disgrace	rompecabezas	puzzle, riddle, slingshot
		rompeolas	breakwater, mole, jetty
gorila	gorilla	salvavidas	life preserver, cowcatcher
idioma	language, tongue, dialect	síntoma	sign, symptom
		sistema	system
la	sixth note on musical scale	sofá	sofa, davenport
mapa	map, chart	telegrama	telegram
mediodía	midday, noon, south, southwind, meridian	tema	theme, subject
		tequila[1]	tequila
		tiralíneas	ruling (or drawing) pen
parabrisa	windshield	trabalenguas	tongue-twister
		tranvía	streetcar

[1] Some dictionaries list this word as masculine, others as feminine!

NOTE: See also some nouns ending in "a" which are sometimes masculine, sometimes feminine as indicated in SECTION X b.

SECTION VII

SOME FEMININE SPANISH NOUNS
WITH ENDINGS USUALLY
CONSIDERED MASCULINE

Spanish	English
la comezón	itch, itching
la mano	hand
la quemazón	burn, fire, excessive heat
la razón	reason, equity, etc.
la sazón	season, maturity, ripeness, flavoring, etc.
la simiente	seed, germ, sperm
la sinrazón	injustice, wrong, injury

SECTION VIII

FEMININE SPANISH NOUNS REQUIRING
THE DEFINITE ARTICLE "EL"
IN THE SINGULAR AND
"LAS" IN THE PLURAL

(Feminine nouns beginning with a stressed "a" or "ha" comprise this category)

Spanish	English	Spanish	English
abra	cove, gap, pass (mountain)	aspa	wing of windmill, blade (propeller), reel (for yarn)
acta	minutes (of a meeting)	asta	horn, antler, mast, pole, flagstaff
agua	water		
águila	eagle	auca	goose
ala	wing, hat brim	aula	schoolroom, lecture hall
alba	dawn	aura	breeze, favor, applause
alma	soul, spirit		
alza	rise, lift (for shoe)	ave	bird, fowl
ama	mistress, owner	aya	child's nurse, governess
anca	haunch, rump	. . . .	
ancla	anchor	haba	large bean, lima bean
ánima	soul, spirit		
ansia	anxiety, anguish, eagerness	habla	speech, language, dialect
ara	altar	hacha	ax, hachet
arca	ark, chest, coffer	hada	fairy
		hambre	hunger, famine, appetite
área	area		
arma	arm, weapon	hampa	underworld
arpa	harp	haya	beech
asa	handle	haz	face, surface

SECTION IX

SPANISH NOUNS ENDING IN IÓN: SOME MASCULINE, SOME FEMININE

NOTE: Spanish nouns ending in "ción" or "sión" are feminine. In the case of nouns ending in "ión" preceded by a consonant other than "c" or "s", some are masculine, some feminine.

MASCULINE

Spanish	English
el camión	truck or wagon
el escorpión	scorpion
el gorrión	sparrow
el sarampión	measles
el turbión	thunderstorm, shower

FEMININE

Spanish	English
la rebelión	rebellion
la reflexión	reflection, meditation
la religión	religion
la reunión	reunion, meeting
la sugestión	suggestion, hint
la unión	union

SECTION X

NOUNS WHICH MAY BE EITHER MASCULINE OR FEMININE WITHOUT CHANGE IN SPELLING

Group a.   NOUNS ENDING IN "ISTA"

(There are many Spanish nouns ending in "ista". The following is a partial and typical list)

Spanish	English	Spanish	English
A		comentarista	commentator
accionista	shareholder, stockholder	comunista	communist
		conferencista	lecturer
activista	activist	conformista	conformist
alarmista	alarmist	congresista	congressman, congresswoman
alienista[1]	alienist		
analista	analyst	contrabandista	smuggler
antagonista	antagonist, opponent	contratista	contractor
artista	artist	**D**	
automovilista	motorist	dentista	dentist
B		deportista	sportsman, sportswoman
bañista	bather		
bautista	Baptist	detallista	retailer, person fond of detail
biciclista	bicyclist		
bolsista	stockbroker	droguista	druggist, cheat, crook
C		**E**	
cambista[1]	banker, money lender	economista[1]	economist
capitalista	capitalist	egoista	selfish person
carterista	pickpocket	electricista[1]	electrician, electrical engineer
coleccionista	collector (of stamps, etc.)		
		enredista	liar, tale-bearer

especialista[1]	specialist

F

fatalista	fatalist
financista[1]	financier
flautista	flute player
fondista	innkeeper

H

huelgista[1]	striker

I

idealista	idealist, dreamer
izquierdista	leftist, radical

J

juerguista	merrymaker

M

malabarista	juggler
maquinista[1]	engineer, machinist, mechanic
mañanista	procrastinator
mayorista[1]	wholesale dealer
motorista	motorist, motorman, motorwoman

N

naturalista	naturalist
novelista	novelist

O

oculista	oculist
optimista	optimist

P

paracaidista	parachutist
pensionista	pensioner, boarder
periodista	journalist, editor or publisher of a newspaper
pesimista	pessimist
prestamista	moneylender
profesionista	professional
protagonista	protagonist
proteccionista	protectionist
proyectista	designer, schemer, planner

R

realista	realist
reformista	reformer

S

socialista	socialist
solista	soloist

T

taxista[1]	taxi driver
telefonista	telephone operator
trampista	cheat, crook, swindler
trapacista	cheat, crook, racketeer

V

violinista	violinist

Group b. NOUNS WITH ENDINGS OTHER THAN "ISTA"

Spanish	English	Spanish	English
A			
acróbata	acrobat	cliente	client, customer
ánade	duck		
anunciante	announcer, advertiser	cofrade	fellow, member of club, etc.
aristócrata	aristocrat	colega	colleague, fellow worker
arte	skill, ability, craft, art		
aspirante	applicant, candidate	comensal	table companion, dinner guest
atleta	athlete		
azteca	Aztec (typical of a race)	compatriota	compatriot, fellow countryman
B			
belga	Belgian (typical of native of a country)	cómplice	accomplice (in crime)
		conferenciante	lecturer
beligerante	belligerent	consorte	consort, mate, companion
C		coparticipe	joint partner
camarada	comrade	creyente	believer
caminante	walker, traveler	criminal	criminal
		cuate	twin, pal, buddy
canadiense	Canadian (typical of native of a country)	**D**	
		danzante	dancer
		delincuente	delinquent
cascarrabias	crab, grouch, ill-tempered person	demandante	plaintiff
		demócrata	democrat
célibe	unmarried person	descendiente	descendant
		déspota	despot, tyrant

dibujante	draftsman, designer
disidente	dissident, protester
dote	dowry

E

emigrante	emigrant
entusiasta	enthusiast
espía	spy
estudiante	student

F

firmante	signer

G

gacetilla	newsmonger, tattletale
gallina	chicken-hearted person
ganzúa	burglar, m. or f. (f. = hook)
guarda	guard, keeper, ticket collector
guía	guide, leader, m. or f. (f. = guidebook)

H

hipócrita	hypocrite
hojaldre	puff pastry
homicida	murderer, murderess

I

idiota	idiot
inmigrante	immigrant
insurgente	insurgent
intérprete	interpreter

intrigante	intriguer, plotter

J

joven	youth, young man or woman

L

lente	lens, m. or f. (lentes m. = eyeglasses)
linde	limit, border, boundary, landmark

M

mar	sea
margen	margin, border, riverbank
menor	minor
modelo	life model

O

ocupante	occupant
oyente	listener, auditor, hearer

P

paciente	patient
paria	outcast
pariente	relative
participante	participant
partícipe	participant
patriota	patriot
penitente	penitent
postulante	petitioner, applicant, candidate

practicante	doctor's assistant, intern
pringue	grease drippings
pro	profit, advantage
profesional	professional
progresita	progressive

R

radio	radio, m. or f. (m. = radius, radium)
reclamante	claimant, complainer
remitente	sender, shipper
reo	culprit, criminal, defendant
reuma	rheumatism
rival	rival, competitor, enemy

S

sinvergüenza	scoundrel, shameless person
siquiatra	alienist, psychiatrist
sobreviviente	survivor
solicitante	solicitor, applicant
suicida	suicide

suplente	substitute
suplicante	supplicant, petitioner

T

terrateniente	landholder
testigo	witness, m. or f. (m. = testimony)
tratante	dealer, tradesman
tunante	rascal, rogue, scamp

V

veleta	weathervane, m. or f. (m. = fickle person)
veraneante	summer resorter, vacationist, tourist
viandante	wayfarer, walker, pedestrian, passerby, vagabond
visitante	caller, visitor

---

[1] Some dictionaries show this word as masculine only, but this distinction is obsolete or rapidly becoming so.

SECTION XI

NOUNS WHICH HAVE A COMMON SPELLING BUT HAVE MEANINGS DEPENDENT UPON GENDER (MASCULINE OR FEMININE)

ATALAYA
  m. = watchman, guard
  f. = lookout post, watchtower

AYA
  m. = tutor, guardian
  f. = governess, child's nurse

CAPITAL
  m. = capital (as funds)
  f. = capital (as a city)

COMA
  m. = coma, stupor
  f. = comma

COMETA
  m. = comet
  f. = kite

CORTE
  m. = cut, cutting edge
  f. = the court

CHIRIPA
  m. = fluke, fortunate chance
  f. = loose riding trousers, cloth used by gauchos

GRANUJA
  m. = (coll.) rogue, gamin, urchin
  f. = loose grapes, grape stone, group of roving boys

GUARDARROPA
  m. or f. = keeper of wardrobe, clothes press, property man (or woman)
  f. = cloakroom

GUÍA
  m. = the guide
  f. = the guidebook

HAZ
  m. = fagot, bundle, bunch
  f. = face, surface

MORAL
  m. = mulberry tree, blackberry bush
  f. = ethics, morale

PAPA
  m. = pope
  f. = potato, fib, lie

PENDIENTE
  m. = earring, pendant
  f. = slope

POLICÍA
  m. = policeman
  f. = police

POSTA
  m. = postboy, messenger, courier
  f. = small bullet, bet, wager
  pl. = buckshot

RATA
  m. = pickpocket
  f. = rat

RAYA
  m. = (sting) ray, skate (a type of fish)
  f. = line, dash, stripe, boundary line, part in the hair

SALVAGUARDIA
  m. = safeguard, protection
  f. = passport, safe-conduct

SECTION XII

NOUNS WHICH HAVE AT LEAST ONE MEANING IN THE PLURAL DIFFERING SUBSTANTIALLY FROM THAT (THOSE) OF THE SINGULAR FORM

Spanish Noun	Singular Meaning(s)	Plural Meaning(s)
A		
abrojo m.	thistle, thorn	reef, hidden rocks in the sea
actualidad f.	present time, nowadays	latest news, fashions or events
afueras f.[1]	(adj. = out, outside)[1]	outskirts, suburbs
alfiler m.	pin, brooch	pin money
altibajo m.	downward thrust (in fencing)	ups and downs, uneven ground
amonestación f.	admonition, advice, warning	marriage bans
andada f.	walk, stroll, hike	track, footprints
aplicación f.	application, effort, diligence	applique (trimming)
arena f.	sand, arena	kidney stones
asiento m.	seat, location, bottom	dregs, sediment
asistencia f.	attendance, help, sitting room	allowance
atención f.	attention, thought, courtesy	business affairs, kindness
B		
barba f.	chin, beard	whiskers
botón m.	bud, button, knob, handle	bellboy (el botones)
brazo m.	arm, branch	day laborers

C

callo m.	callus, corn (on foot)	tripe (food)
candileja f.	small oil lamp	footlights (of a stage)
celo m.	zeal, ardor, envy	jealousy, suspicion
circunstantes m.[1]	(adj. = surrounding, present)[1]	bystanders, audience
cobre m.	copper, copper utensils	brass musical instruments
coral m.	coral	coral beads

D

| desperdicio m. | waste, extravagance | leftovers, garbage, residue |

E

efecto m.	effect, result, end, purpose	goods, personal property
elástico m.	elastic, wire spring	suspenders
entrada f.	entrance, gate, opening, etc.	cash receipts
esposa f.	wife	handcuffs
existencia f.	existence	goods, stock on hand
expresión f.	expression, utterance	regards

F

facción f.	faction, band, party, battle	features
fantasía f.	fantasy, whim, imagination	string of pearls
fatiga f.	fatigue, toil	hardships
felicidad f.	happiness	congratulations!
fondo m.	bottom, background	funds (money)
frío m.	cold	chills and fever

G

gemelo m.	twin	twins, binoculars, cuff links
gestión f.	action, maneuver	negotiations
gotera f.	leak, eaves, trough	surroundings, outskirts
grillo m.	cricket, sprout, shoot	fetters, hindrance
guarnición f.	adornment, trimming	trappings, harness

H

haber m.	credit	goods, cash, assets
hierro m.	iron, weapon, etc.	chains, handcuffs
honra f.	honor, reputation	obsequies, funeral rites

I

ingreso m.	entrance	receipts, profits, revenue

L

lente m. and f.	lens	m. eyeglasses

M

macarrón m.	macaroon	macaroni
máscara f.	mask	masquerade
memoria f.	memory, memoir, note, etc.	regards, memoirs
mies f.	ripe grain, harvest	fields of grain
musa f.	Muse, poetry	fine arts

O

orín m.	rust	urine

P

padre m.	father	parents, ancestors
paloma f.	dove, pigeon, mild person	whitecaps

papera f.	goiter	mumps
parte f.	part, share, place	qualities
patilla f.	small foot or paw	sideburns
pelillo m.	short fine hair	trouble, nuisance
perejil m.	parsley	frippery, fancy clothes
posibles m.[1]	(adj. = possible)[1]	goods, property, means
prenda f.	pawn, pledge, token, etc.	talents, good qualities
prisión f.	prison, imprisonment	shackles, chains

Q

quilate m.	carat	qualities, degree of purity

R

recuerdo m.	recollection, souvenir	regards
recurso m.	recourse, appeal	means, resources
requerimiento m.	requisition, summons, etc.	amorous advances, insinuations
resto m.	rest, remainder, etc.	remains
roseta f.	rosette, small rose	popcorn

S

seña f.	sign, mark, password	address
sobra f.	surplus, excess	leftovers, leavings

T

tabla, f.	board, plank, slab	tie (game), stage

V

valor m.	value, price, valor	stocks, bonds
víspera f.	eve, evening before	vespers

---

[1] Used as an adjective in the singular and plural forms, but as a noun in the plural only

SECTION XIII

SPANISH NOUNS WHICH MAY SEEM TO THE ENGLISH-SPEAKING PERSON TO HAVE INAPPROPRIATE GENDER

Group a.   MASCULINE NOUNS

Spanish	English meaning	Spanish	English meaning
el aborto	abortion, miscarriage	el naci- miento	birth
el arrullo	lullaby, cooing	el parto	birth
el brazalete	bracelet	el pecho	breast, bosom
el bucle	curl, ringlet	el pendiente	earring
el collar	necklace	el pezón	nipple
el corsé	corset	el refajo	underskirt, short skirt
el chiche	breast, teat, wet nurse	el rulo	curler (for hair)
el gorro	bonnet	el seno	breast, bosom
el malparto	abortion, miscarriage	el traje	dress
el menstruo	menstruation	el útero	uterus, womb
		el vestido	dress

Group b.   FEMININE NOUNS

Spanish	English meaning	Spanish	English meaning
la barba	beard (or chin)	la gorra	cap
las barbas	whiskers	la guar- diamarina	midshipman
la camisa	shirt	las patillas	sideburns
la camiseta	undershirt (for men)	la próstata	prostate
la corbata	necktie		

SECTION XIV

REFLEXIVE VERBS WHICH HAVE
AT LEAST ONE MEANING DIFFERING
SUBSTANTIALLY FROM THAT OF
THE NON-REFLEXIVE FORM

NOTES: There are many reflexive Spanish verbs which have meanings all of which are readily understood if one knows the meanings of the non-reflexive form. These do not appear in the list presented here. The verb **sorprender** ("to surprise"), **sorprenderse** ("to be surprised") is clearly of the type excluded. The verb **secar** ("to dry"), **secarse** ("to dry oneself, to become dry, to dry up, to become withered, to become thin") is typical of a borderline case because the last two meanings might not always be recognized as derivatives of "to dry". (It was omitted from the presented list.) There are many of these borderline cases not included herein.

A good many of the verbs listed have a great variety of meanings. In these cases a selection (adequate to show the contrast between the reflexive and non-reflexive forms) was made, omitting other meanings to conserve space.

Entries marked with an asterisk (*) show only the "unexpected" meaning(s), whereas the reflexive form is at times used in the same or nearly same sense as the non-reflexive form. For example, **dañar** ("to hurt, harm, etc.") can in the reflexive form **dañarse,** have the meanings "to hurt oneself", "to be harmed", etc., but also has the meanings "to rot" or "to spoil". The asterisk marking is somewhat arbitrary and the student may find additional cases to which he would choose to apply the marking.

Verb	Meaning(s) Non-reflexive form	Meaning(s) Reflexive form
ABONAR(SE)	to pay, credit with, fertilize (soil)	to subscribe
ABRUMAR(SE)	to crush, trouble, annoy	to become foggy
ABSTRAER(SE)	to abstract, remove, withdraw	to be lost in thought
ACENTUAR(SE)	to accent, emphasize	to become worse (as an illness)
ACORDAR(SE)	to arrange, decide, agree upon	to remember

ACORTAR(SE)	to shorten	to shrink, be bashful
ADMIRAR(SE)	to admire	to wonder, be astonished
AFANAR(SE)	to urge, press, toil	to worry, be eager*
AGAZAPAR(SE)	to nab, seize (a person)	to crouch, squat
ALUMBRAR(SE)	to light, illuminate, give birth	to get tipsy
ANTICIPAR(SE)	to anticipate, pay in advance, lend	to arrive ahead of time, get ahead of
APARTAR(SE)	to separate, remove, divide	to withdraw, step aside, go away
APROPIAR(SE)	to fit, adapt	to confiscate, take possession of
ARRASAR(SE)	to level, raze	to clear up (said of sky)
ARREGLAR(SE)	to arrange, adjust, fix	to dress up, settle differences
ARRESTAR(SE)	to arrest	to dare, venture
ARRIMAR(SE)	to place near, to lay aside	to lean on, get near, seek shelter
ASENTAR(SE)	to set, write down, hone	to settle
ATAR(SE)	to tie, fasten	to be puzzled*
ATRANCAR(SE)	to bolt, fasten with a bolt	to get cramped, obstructed
ATROPELLAR(SE)	to run over, knock down	to rush, rush through
BUFAR(SE)	to snort, puff with anger	to swell or bulge (as a wall)

CERNER(SE)	to sift, drizzle	to hover (as bird or plane)
COLAR(SE)	to filter, bleach	to sneak in or out
CONDENAR(SE)	to condemn, sentence	to be damned
CONDUCIR(SE)	to conduct, lead, drive (a car)	to behave, act
CORREGIR(SE)	to correct, punish	to mend one's ways
CORTAR(SE)	to cut, interrupt, shut off	to be ashamed, to sour (re milk)*
CRECER(SE)	to grow, increase	to swell (re river), become or feel important
CUARTEAR(SE)	to divide into quarters	to crack (e.g., walls), to back down, go back on one's word
CHIFLAR(SE)	to whistle, hiss	to lose one's head, become crazy
CHILLAR(SE)	to scream, hiss	to be offended
DAÑAR(SE)	to hurt, harm, damage	to spoil or rot*
DAR(SE)	to give, hit, emit	to give up
DECLARAR(SE)	to declare, affirm, testify	to propose, declare one's love
DEMUDAR(SE)	to change, disguise	to change facial expression, to turn pale
DERRIBAR(SE)	to knock down, overthrow	to lie down, throw oneself down
DERRUMBAR(SE)	to fling down	to crumble away, topple over
DESBORDAR(SE)	to overflow, flood	to get over-excited*
DESCABEZAR(SE)	to behead, cut off the tip	to rack one's brain*

DESCOSER(SE)	to rip, unsew	to talk too much or indiscreetly*
DESEMPEÑAR(SE)	to recover, redeem, carry out	to get out of debt
DESMAYAR(SE)	to dismay, be dismayed, lose courage	to faint
DESOLAR(SE)	to lay waste, ruin	to grieve, be in anguish
DESPEDIR(SE)	to discharge, throw off	to take leave, say goodbye
DIBUJAR(SE)	to draw, portray	to appear, show
DISIPAR(SE)	to dissipate, scatter, squander	to vanish
DISPARAR(SE)	to shoot, discharge	to run away, dart out
DISPONER(SE)	to arrange, put in order	to get ready, make one's will
DISTRAER(SE)	to divert, amuse	to have a good time, to be inattentive*
DOBLAR(SE)	to bend, fold, double	to bend over, stoop, yield
DOBLEGAR(se)	to bend, fold, double	to bend over, stoop, yield
ELEVAR(SE)	to raise, lift	to go up, scar, climb
EMPACHAR(SE)	to stuff, to cause indigestion	to get upset, get embarrassed*
EMPAQUETAR(SE)	to pack, package	to dress up
ENARBOLAR(SE)	to lift, raise	to rear, balk
ENCAJAR(SE)	to thrust in, fit into	to meddle*
ENCAMINAR(SE)	to direct, guide	to go, to start out (on a road)

ENCARAMAR(SE)	to raise, extol	to climb, to climb or perch upon
ENCERRAR(SE)	to enclose, lock up	to go into seclusion*
ENJALBEGAR(SE)	to whitewash	to paint (one's face)
ENNEGRECER(SE)	to blacken, darken	to become cloudy*
ENTERAR(SE)	to inform	to learn, find out
ENTRAMPAR(SE)	to trap, ensnare	to run into debt*
ENTREGAR(SE)	to deliver, hand over	to surrender, give up, devote oneself
ENVICIAR(SE)	to vitiate, corrupt	to become addicted (to)
ERGUIR(SE)	to erect, set upright	to become proud and haughty
ESFUMAR(SE)	to shade, tone down	to disappear
ESMERAR(SE)	to polish, clean	to strive, take great care
ESPARCIR(SE)	to scatter, spread	to relax, amuse oneself
ESPIGAR(SE)	to glean, grow spikes (re grain)	to grow tall and slender
ESTILAR(SE)	to use, be accustomed to use	to be in style (of clothes)
EXALTAR(SE)	to exalt, glorify, praise	to get excited or emotionally upset
EXCEDER(SE)	to exceed, overdo	to misbehave
EXHALAR(SE)	to exhale, emit, give off	to evaporate, run away
EXTRAVIAR(SE)	to lead astray, misplace	to get lost or stranded, miss the road
FIGURAR(SE)	to figure, represent	to imagine, think
FIJAR(SE)	to fix, fasten, establish	to settle, to pay attention

FLETAR(SE)	to charter, freight	to run or slip away
FORMALIZAR(SE)	to legalize, make official	to settle down, become serious
FRANQUEAR(SE)	to exempt, frank, make grants	to disclose one's thoughts or feelings
GRANULAR(SE)	to granulate	to break out with pimples*
HACER(SE)	to do, make	to become
HOLGAR(SE)	to rest, loaf	to be glad, relax, have a good time
HURTAR(SE)	to steal, rob, pilfer	to withdraw, hide
INFORMAR(SE)	to inform, report	to find out*
INGERIR(SE)	to inject, insert	to interfere, meddle
INMISCUIR(SE)	to mix	to interfere, meddle
INMUTAR(SE)	to alter, change	to show emotion by blushing or paling
INSULTAR(SE)	to insult	to be seized with a fit
INTERNAR(SE)	to intern, confine	to penetrate, go into the interior
LARGAR(SE)	to loosen, let go	to slip away, leave
LEVANTAR(SE)	to raise	to get up
MALOGRAR(SE)	to waste, lose, miss	to fail, turn out badly
MANEJAR(SE)	to manage, drive (a car)	to move about, get around (after illness, etc.)

MARCHAR(SE)	to march, walk, parade	to go away
MAREAR(SE)	to navigate, sail, annoy	to get seasick, nauseated, or dizzy
METER(SE)	to put, insert, smuggle, cause (fear, etc.)	to interfere, meddle*
MOSQUEAR(SE)	to brush (flies) away, whip	to show resentment
MUDAR(SE)	to change, remove, molt	to change one's habits, abode, or clothes
PARECER(SE)	to seem, appear, show up	to look alike
PASAR(SE)	to pass, cross, exceed	to transfer, get over-ripe*
PEGAR(SE)	to hit, paste (glue), sew on, infect	to stick, cling, to be catching
PERDER(SE)	to lose, ruin, miss	to get spoiled, go astray*
PERECER(SE)	to perish, die	to long for
PINTAR(SE)	to paint, depict, imagine	to put on makeup
PONER(SE)	to put	to dress, put on clothing
PRODUCIR(SE)	to produce, yield	to explain oneself, to break out
PROMETER(SE)	to promise	to become engaged
PRONUNCIAR(SE)	to pronounce, utter	to rebel
QUERER(SE)	to want, desire love	to love each other

QUITAR(SE)	to remove, take away	to undress, take off clothing
RECATAR(SE)	to cover, conceal	to be timid or cautious, to shun
RECOGER(SE)	to get, gather, tighten, shelter	to retire, go home, withdraw
REDUCIR(SE)	to reduce, convert (into)	to adapt oneself*
REGALAR(SE)	to give, entertain, please	to live a pleasant easy life
REHACER(SE)	to remake, repair	to rally, regain one's strength
RELAJAR(SE)	to relax, release from a vow	to become lax, get a hernia*
REPICAR(SE)	to chime, ring, chop fine	to boast, be conceited
REPLEGAR(SE)	to fold, pleat	to retreat, fall back
REPONER(SE)	to replace, restore, reply	to recover health or fortune, become calm
REPOSAR(SE)	to rest, lie buried	to settle (re sediment)
REPRESENTAR(SE)	to represent, state, show, act	to imagine, picture oneself
REQUEMAR(SE)	to dry up, overcook, burn	to get overheated, tanned, sunburned
RESFRIAR(SE)	to cool, chill	to catch cold*
RESPALDAR(SE)	to endorse, guarantee	to lean back
RESUMIR(SE)	to sum up	to be reduced or condensed
RETORCER(SE)	to twist, distort	to squirm, wriggle

SABOREAR(SE)	to savor, season, enjoy	to smack one's lips*
SAZONAR(SE)	to season, flavor	to ripen, mature*
SECRETEAR(SE)	to whisper	to whisper to each other
SEÑALAR(SE)	to mark, determine, signal	to distinguish oneself
SOLAZAR(SE)	to console, cheer, comfort	to seek relaxation, to enjoy oneself
SONAR(SE)	to sound, ring	to blow one's nose
SUMAR(SE)	to add, sum up	to join
TOCAR(SE)	to touch, play (instrument), ring	to fix one's hair, to go a little crazy
TRANSPONER(SE)	to transpose, transplant, go beyond	to hide from view, go below the horizon
VIOLENTAR(SE)	to force, break into	to get angry*
VISLUMBRAR(SE)	to catch glimpse of, guess	to be faintly visible, glimmer

SECTION XV

PARTS OF THE HUMAN BODY
(Partes del cuerpo humano)

Group a. ENGLISH TO SPANISH

English	Spanish	English	Spanish
A		body	el cuerpo
abdomen (belly)	el abdomen, el vientre	bone	el hueso
Adam's apple	la manzana de Adán	bosom (breast)	el seno
ankle	el tobillo	brain	el cerebro, el seso
anus	el ano, el orificio	breast (bosom)	el seno
areola	la aréola	bronchial tube	el bronquio
arm	el brazo	bust	el busto
armpit	el sobaco	buttocks	las nalgas
artery	la arteria	**C**	
B		calf	la pantorrilla
back	la espalda	cheek	la mejilla
backbone (spinal column)	el espinazo, la columna vertebral	cheekbone	el pómulo
		chest	el pecho
beard	la barba	chin	la barba
belly (abdomen)	el abdomen, el vientre, la barriga	cornea	la córnea
bladder	la vejiga	**D**	
blood	la sangre	dimple	el hoyuelo

E

ear	la oreja, el oído
eardrum	el tímpano
elbow	el codo
esophagus	el esófago
eye	el ojo
eyebrow	la ceja
eyelash	la pestaña
eyelid	el párpado

F

face	la cara, el rostro
figure	el talle
finger	el dedo
fingernail	la uña
fist	el puño
foot	el pie
forearm	el antebrazo
forehead	la frente

G

gall bladder	la vejiga de la bilis, vesícula biliar
genitals	los órganos genitales
gland	la glándula
groin	la ingle

gums	las encías

H

hand	la mano
hair	el pelo
head	la cabeza
heart	el corazón
heel	el talón
hip	la cadera

I

insides	el coleto
instep	el empeine
intestine	la tripa
iris	el iris

J

jaw	la quijada, la mandíbula
joint	la juntura, la coyuntura

K

kidney	el riñón
knee	la rodilla
knee cap (patella)	la rótula, la choquezuela
knuckle	el nudillo

L

lap	el regazo
larynx	la laringe

leg	la pierna	rib	la costilla
lip	el labio		
liver	el hígado	**S**	
lobe of ear	el lobo,	shin	la espinilla
	el lóbulo	shoulder	el hombro
lung	el pulmón	shoulder blade	la espaldilla
		sideburns	las patillas
M		skeleton	el esqueleto
moustache	el bigote	skin	la piel,
mouth	la boca		el cutis
muscle	el músculo	skull	el cráneo,
			la calavera
N		sole (of	la planta
navel	el ombligo	foot)	
neck	el cuello,	spine (spinal	el espinazo,
	la nuca	column)	la columna
			vertebral
nerve	el nervio		
nipple	el pezón	spleen	el bazo
nose	la nariz	stomach	el estómago
O		**T**	
organ	el órgano	temple	la sien
		tendon	el tendón
P		thigh	el muslo
palate	el paladar	throat	la garganta
pancreas	el páncreas	thumb	el pulgar
patella	la rótula, la	tiptoes	las puntillas
	choquezuela	toe	el dedo
prostate	la próstata		del pie
		toenail	la uña del
R			dedo del pie
retina	la retina	tongue	la lengua

tonsil	la amígdala	**W**	
tooth	el diente	waist	la cintura, el talle
trachea	la tráquea		
trunk	el tronco	whiskers	las barbas
V		windpipe	la tráquea
		womb	el útero
vein	la vena	wrist	la muñeca

Group b.   SPANISH TO ENGLISH

Spanish	English	Spanish	English

A

Spanish	English
el abdomen (el vientre)	abdomen, belly
el ano (el orificio)	anus
la aréola	areola
la arteria	artery

B

la barba	chin, beard, (pl. = whiskers)
la barriga	belly
el bazo	spleen
el bigote	moustache
la boca	mouth
el brazo (antebrazo)	arm (forearm)
el bronquio	bronchial tube
el busto	bust

C

la cabeza	head
la cadera	hip
la calavera	skull
la cara (el rostro)	face
la ceja	eyebrow
el cerebro (el seso)	brain
la cintura	waist
el codo	elbow
el coleto	insides
la columna vertebral (el espinazo)	backbone, spinal column
el corazón	heart
la córnea	cornea
la costilla	rib
el cráneo	skull

el cuello (la nuca)	neck	el hombro	shoulder
		el hoyuelo	dimple
el cuerpo	body	el hueso	bone
el cutis	skin		

D

el dedo	finger
el dedo del pie	toe
el diente (postizo)	tooth (false)

I

la ingle	groin
el iris	iris

J

la juntura (la coyuntura)	joint

E

el empeine	instep
las encías	gums (of the mouth)
el esófago	esophagus
la espalda	back
la espaldilla	shoulder blade
el espinazo	spine
el esqueleto	skeleton
el estómago	stomach

L

el labio	lip
la laringe	larynx
la lengua	tongue
el lóbulo (el lobo)	lobe (of ear)

M

la mano	hand
la manzana de Adán	Adam's apple
la mejilla	cheek
la muñeca	wrist
el muslo	thigh
el músculo	muscle

F

la frente	forehead

G

la garganta	throat
la glándula	gland

N

las nalgas	buttocks
la nariz	nose

H

el hígado	liver

el nervio	nerve		el pulgar	thumb
el nudillo	knuckle		el pulmón	lung

O

			las puntillas	tiptoes
el ojo	eye		el puño	fist

el ombligo (centro, medio)	navel

Q

la quijada (la mandíbula)	jaw

la oreja (el oído)	ear

R

los órganos genitales	genitals

el regazo	lap
la retina	retina
el riñón	kidney
la rodilla	knee

P

el paladar	palate
el páncreas	pancreas
la pantorilla	calf
el párpado	eyelid
las patillas	sideburns

la rótula (la choquezuela)	patella, knee cap

S

la sangre	blood
el pecho	chest, breast, bosom

el seno	bosom, breast
el pelo	hair
la sien	temple
la piel (el cutis)	skin
el sobaco	armpit

T

la pestaña	eyelash
el pezón	nipple
la pierna	leg
el pie	foot
la planta	sole of foot
el pómulo	cheekbone
la próstata	prostate

el talón	heel
el talle	figure, waist
el tendón	tendon
el tímpano	ear drum
el tobillo	ankle
la amígdala	tonsil

la tráquea	trachea, windpipe	el útero	womb

V

la tripa (el intestino)	intestine	la vejiga	bladder
		la vejiga de la bilis (vesícula biliar)	gall bladder
el tronco	trunk		

U

la uña del dedo (del pie)	fingernail (toe nail)	la vena	vein

Group c.   SKIN CONDITIONS
(Algunos aspectos de la piel)

English	Spanish	Spanish	English
birthmark	el estigma, la marca de nacimiento	el callo	corn
		la cicatriz	scar
boil	el divieso, el furúnculo	la contusión	bruise
		la cortadura	cut
bruise	la contusión	el divieso, el furúnculo	boil
bunion	el juanete		
burn	la quemadura	el estigma, la marca de nacimiento	birthmark
corn	el callo		
cut	la cortadura	el grano	pimple
freckle	la peca	la herida	wound
mole	el lunar	el juanete	bunion
pimple	el grano	el lunar	mole
rash	el salpullido, el sarpullido, el hervor de sangre	la peca	freckle
		la quemadura	burn
scar	la cicatriz		

English	Spanish	Spanish	English
wart	la verruga	el salpullido, el sarpullido, el hervor de sangre	rash
wound	la herida		
		la verruga	wart

SECTION XVI
RELATIVES AND WORDS ASSOCIATED
WITH FAMILY RELATIONSHIPS

Group a. DIRECT RELATIONSHIPS

English	Spanish	English	Spanish
parents	los padres	second cousin	el primo segundo
husband	el esposo	grandfather	el abuelo
wife	la esposa	grandmother	la abuela
father	el papá, padre	grandson	el nieto
mother	la mamá, madre	grand-daughter	la nieta
son	el hijo	great grand-father	el bisabuelo
daughter	la hija		
brother	el hermano	great grand-mother	la bisabuela
sister	la hermana		
uncle	el tío	great grandson	el biznieto
aunt	la tía		
nephew	el sobrino	great grand-daughter	la biznieta
niece	la sobrina		
cousin	el primo, la prima	great-great grandfather (- -grandson, etc.)	el tatarabuelo, (el tataranieto, etc.)
first cousin	el primo hermano		

Group b. SECONDARY FAMILY RELATIONSHIPS
OR ASSOCIATED TERMS

English	Spanish	English	Spanish
ancestor	el antepasado	baby	el bebé, la criatura, el nene, la nena

best man	el padrino de boda	foster father	el padre adoptivo
birth	el nacimiento, el parto	foster mother	la madre adoptiva
birthday	el cumpleaños	foster son	el hijo de leche
boy	el niño, el muchacho, el chico	foster daughter	la hija de leche
bride	la desposada, (la novia)	foster brother	el hermano de leche
bridegroom	el desposado, (el novio)	foster sister	la hermana de leche
bridesmaid (maid of honor)	la madrina de boda	girl	la niña, la muchacha, la chica
child	el niño, la niña, el hijo, la hija	godfather	el padrino
		godmother	la madrina
		godson	el ahijado
childhood	la niñez	goddaughter	la ahijada
childless	sin hijos	guardian	el tutor
divorce	el divorcio, el descasamiento	half-breed, half-caste	el mestizo
		heredity	la herencia
divorcé	el esposo divorciado	honeymoon	la luna de miel, el viaje de novios
divorcee	la esposa divorciada		
family tree	el árbol genealógico	infant	el infante, el bebé, el nene, la nena, la criatura
fatherhood	la paternidad		
fiancé	el novio		
fiancée	la novia	infancy	la infancia
foster parents	los padres adoptivos		

"in-law" relationships:

father-in-law	el suegro
mother-in-law	la suegra
son-in-law	el yerno, el hijo político
daughter-in-law	la nuera
brother-in-law	el cuñado
sister-in-law	la cuñada
lover	el amante, la amante
marriage	el casamiento, el enlace
married	casado, unido
married couple	el matrimonio
motherhood	la maternidad

orphan	el huérfano
relationships	el parentesco
stepfather	el padrastro
stepmother	la madrastra
stepson	el hijastro
stepdaughter	la hijastra
stepbrother (half-brother)	el hermanastro, el medio hermano
stepsister (half-sister)	la hermanastra, la media hermana
twin (twins)	el gemelo (los gemelos)
wedding	la boda, las nupcias, el casamiento, el enlace
widower	el viudo
widow	la viuda

SECTION XVII

COLORS (ENGLISH - SPANISH)

English	Spanish	English	Spanish
azure	azur, azul celeste	indigo blue	añil, azul índigo, azul turquí
black	negro		
blue	azul	lavender	lila, morado claro
baby blue	azul claro		
dark[1] blue	azul obscuro	lemon yellow	cetrino
light[1] blue	azul claro	lilac	lila
navy blue	azul marino		
sky blue	azul celeste	maroon	marrón, rojo obscuro
(see also "cerulean" and "indigo")			
		mauve	malvo
brown	café, tostado, castaño	orange	color de naranja, anaranjado
dark brown	moreno, café obscuro		
		pink	rosa
cerulean (a blue)	cerúleo	purple	púrpura, morado
crimson	carmín, carmesí	red	rojo, encarnado, colorado
gray	gris		
dark gray	pardo obscuro	rose	rosa
green	verde	turquoise	turquesa
bottle green	verde botella	violet	violado
sea green	verde mar	white	blanco
		yellow	amarillo

---

[1] Colors are frequently modified by "**obscuro**" to mean "dark" or "**claro**" to mean "light".

SECTION XVIII
GIVEN NAMES (ENGLISH-SPANISH)

The following is a list of the most frequently used given names. Surprisingly few sources provide these "first" names.

Group a. MASCULINE NAMES

English	Spanish	English	Spanish
A		**B**	
Aaron	Aarón	Bartholomew	Bartolomé
Abraham	Abrahán	Basil	Basilio
Adam	Adán	Benedict	Benedicto, Benito
Adolph	Adolfo		
Adrian	Adrián	Benjamin	Benjamín
Albert	Alberto	Bernard	Bernardo
Alexander	Alejandro	Bertram	Bertrán
Alexis	Alejo	Bruno	Bruno
Alfred	Alfredo	**C**	
Alphonse	Alfonso	Calvin	Calvino
Alvin	Aluino	Casper	Gaspar
Ambrose	Ambrosio	Cecil	Cecilio
Andrew	Andrés	Charles (Chuck)	Carlos
Anthony (Tony)	Antonio	Christian	Cristiano
Archibald	Archibaldo	Christopher	Cristóbal
Arnold	Arnaldo	Claudius, Claude	Claudio
Arthur	Arturo	Clement	Clemente
Augustine	Agustín	Conrad	Conrado

Constantine	Constantino
Cornelius	Cornelio
Cyril	Cirilo

D

Daniel	Daniel
David	David
Dennis	Dionisio
Dominic	Domingo
Donald	Donato

E

Edgar	Edgar
Edmund, Edmond	Edmundo
Edward	Eduardo
Elliot	Helio, Elio
Emil	Emilio
Emmanuel	Manuel
Eric	Enrique
Ernest	Ernesto
Eugene	Eugenio

F

Felix	Félix
Ferdinand	Fernando
Francis	Francisco
Frank	Pancho, Paco
Frederick (Fred)	Federico

G

Gabriel	Gabriel
Geoffrey	Geofredo
George	Jorge
Gerald (Jerry), Gerard	Gerardo
Gilbert	Gilberto
Godfrey	Godofredo
Gregory	Gregorio
Gustave	Gustavo
Guy	Guido

H

Harold	Haraldo
Hector	Héctor
Henry, Harry	Enrique
Herbert	Heriberto, Heberto
Hilary	Hilario
Homer	Homero
Horace, Horatio	Horacio
Hubert	Huberto, Umberto
Hugh	Hugo

I

Isaac	Isaac
Isaiah	Isaías

J

Jack	Juanito
Jacob	Jacobo
James (Jim)	Jaime, Diego
Jasper	Gaspar
Jeffrey	Geofredo
Jerome (Jerry)	Jerónimo
Jesse	Jaime
Joachim	Joaquín
Joe	Pepe
John	Juan
Jonathan	Jonatán
Joseph	José
Jules, Julius	Julio
Julian	Julián

L

Lambert	Lamberto
Lancelot	Lanzarote
Lawrence	Lorenzo
Leon, Leo	León
Leonard	Leonardo
Leopold	Leopoldo
Lionel	Leonel
Louis	Luis
Lucius	Lucio
Luke	Lucas
Luther	Lutero

M

Manuel	Manuel
Mark, Marcus	Marco
Martin	Martín
Matthew	Mateo
Maurice	Mauricio
Michael (Mike)	Miguel
Moses	Moisés

N

Nathan	Natán
Nathaniel	Nataniel
Nicholas (Nick)	Nicolás
Noah	Noé
Noel	Noel

O

Oliver	Oliverio
Orlando	Orlando
Oscar	Oscar
Oswald	Oswaldo
Otto	Otón

P

Patrick (Pat)	Patricio
Paul	Pablo
Peter	Pedro
Philip	Felipe

Q

Quenten, Quintin	Quintín

R

Ralph, Raphael	Rafael
Randolph	Randolfo
Raymond (Ray)	Raimundo, Ramón
Reginald	Reginaldo
Reuben	Rubén
Reynold	Reinaldo
Richard (Dick)	Ricardo
Robert (Bob)	Roberto
Roderick	Rodrigo
Roger	Rogelio
Roland	Rolando, Orlando
Ronald	Renaldo
Rudolph	Rodolfo
Ruben	Rubén
Rufus	Rufo
Rupert	Ruperto

S

Samuel (Sam)	Samuel
Sebastian	Sebastián
Simon	Simón
Solomon	Salomón
Stephen (Steve)	Esteban
Stewart	Estuardo
Sylvester	Silvestre

T

Terence	Terencio
Thaddeus	Tadeo
Theobald	Teobaldo
Theodore (Ted)	Teodoro
Thomas (Tom)	Tomás
Timothy	Timoteo
Titus	Tito
Tobias	Tobías

V

Valentine	Valentín
Vergil, Virgil	Virgilio
Victor	Víctor
Vincent	Vicente

W

Walter	Gualterio
Wilfred	Wilfredo
William (Bill)	Guillermo

Z

Zachariah, Zachary	Zacarías

Group b. FEMININE NAMES

English	Spanish	English	Spanish
		Carmen	Carmen
A		Caroline, Carolyn	Carolina
Adelaide, Adeline	Adelaida	Catherine, Kate, Cathy	Catalina
Adele	Adela		
Agnes	Inés	Cecilia, Cecily	Cecilia
Aileen	Elena		
Alberta	Alberta	Celeste	Celeste
Alice	Alicia	Celia	Celia
Alma	Alma	Charlotte	Carlota
Amanda	Amanda	Christine	Cristina
Amelia	Amalia	Clara, Clare, Clarice, Clarissa	Clara
Angela, Angeline	Angela, Angelina		
Anita	Anita	Claudia	Claudia
Ann, Anne, Anna	Ana	Clementine	Clementina
		Cleo	Cleopatra
Antoinette	Antonia	Connie, Constance	Constanza, Constancia
B		Cornelia	Cornelia
Barbara	Bárbara	**D**	
Beatrice	Beatriz		
Bertha	Berta	Deborah	Déborah
Betty (Betsy)	Chavela, Belita	Dianna, Diane	Diana
Blanche	Blanca	Dolores	Dolores
C		Dora	Dora
Camille	Camila	Dorothea, Dorothy	Dorotea

E

Edith	Edith
Eileen	Elena
Eleanor	Eleanora
Elizabeth (Betty), Lisa	Isabel, Elisa
Ellen	Elena
Eloise	Eloisa
Elsa	Elsa
Elsie	Elisa
Elvira	Elvira
Emily	Emilia
Emma	Ema
Esther	Ester
Eugenia, Eugenie	Eugenia
Eve	Eva

F

Felicia	Felisa
Flora	Flora
Florence (Flo)	Florencia
Frances	Francisca

G

Genevieve	Genoveva
Georgia	Georgina
Geraldine	Geraldina
Gertrude	Gertrudis
Gladys	Gladys

Gloria	Gloria
Grace	Engracia
Greta	Margarita

H

Harriet	Enriqueta
Helen, Helena	Elena
Henrietta, Henriette	Enriqueta
Hilda	Hilda
Hope	Esperanza
Hortense	Hortencia

I

Irene	Irene
Iris	Iris
Irma	Irma
Isabel	Isabel

J

Jacqueline (Jackie)	Jacoba
Jane, Janet	Juana
Jeanette, Jennie	Juanita
Joan, Joanne	Juana
Josephine	Josefina
Judith, Judy	Judit
Julia, Julie	Julia

Juliette	Julieta
Justine	Justina

K

Katherine, Kate, Kathryn, Kathy, Kay, Kitty	Catalina

L

Laura	Laura
Lena	Elena
Leonora	Leonor
Lillian	Lilian
Lily	Lilí
Linda	Linda
Lisa	Isabel
Lola	Lola
Loretta	Loreta
Louise	Luisa
Lucia, Lucille, Lucy	Lucía

M

Magdalen	Magdalena
Marcella	Marcela
Margaret (Peggy)	Margarita
Marguerite, Margo	Margarita
Marion	Mariana

Marilyn, Marjorie, Marjory	María
Martha	Marta
Mary, Maria, Maric	María
Matilda	Matilde
Mercedes	Mercedes
Miriam	Miriam
Mollie, Molly	Mariquita, Maruja
Monica, Mona	Mónica

N

Nancy	Nancy
Naomi	Noemi
Natalie	Natalia
Nellie	Nelly
Nina	Nina
Nora	Nora
Norma	Norma

O

Olga	Olga
Olive	Oliva

P

Pamela	Pamela
Patricia (Pat)	Patricia
Paula, Pauline	Paula, Paulina
Pearl	Perla

Penelope	Penélope	Sophia, Sophie	Sofía
Phyllis	Filis	Stella	Estela
Pilar	Pilar	Susan, Susanna	Susana
Priscilla	Priscila		
Prudence	Prudencia	Sylvia	Silvia

R

Rachel	Raquel	Teresa, Theresa	Teresa
Ramona	Ramona		
Rebecca	Rebeca	Theodora	Teodora
Regina	Regina		

U

Rita	Rita	Ursula	Ursula
Roberta	Roberta		

V

Rosalie, Rosalyn, Rosanne	Rosalía, Rosana	Valerie	Valeria
		Veronica	Verónica
Rose	Rosa	Victoria, Vicki	Victoria
Rosemary	Rosa María		
Ruth	Ruth	Viola, Violet	Violeta

S

		Virginia	Virginia
Sabrina	Sabrina	Vivian	Viviana
Sara, Sarah (Sally)	Sara		

SECTION XIX

EXAMPLES OF SPANISH WORDS
REQUIRING THE DIERESIS MARK

NOTE: When the letter "u" in Spanish appears in conjunction with another vowel it is sometimes desired to have the "u" pronounced separately, rather than as a diphthong. If the accent is to fall on the "u", then the accent mark is adequate to yield the separate sound (e.g., **baúl**). If the accent is on a letter other than the "u", the dieresis mark (··) is used to indicate the separate sound for the "u" (e.g., **bilingüe**).

Spanish	English
agüero m.	augury, prediction, omen
ambigüedad f.	ambiguity
antigüedad f.	antiquity
argüir	to argue
bilingüe (adj.)	bilingual
cigüeña f.	stork, crane, winch
cigüeñal m.	crank shaft
cigüeño m.	male stork
cigüete f.	variety of small grape
desagüe m.	channel, drain, drainage
desvergüenza f.	impudence, insolence, shamelessness
güeldo m.	shrimp, clams (for bait)
güepil, güipil m.	rich cloth worn by Indian women
güero (adj.)	blond
güira f.	calabash tree
lengüecita f.	small tongue

lengüeta f.	small tongue, epiglottis, etc.
lengüetada f.	act of licking
lingüista f.	linguist
lingüística f.	linguistics
lingüístico (adj.)	linguistic
pingüe (adj.)	abundant, fat, greasy
pingüino m.	penguin
ungüentario (adj.)	sweet-scented
ungüento m.	ointment, salve
vergüenza f.	shame, modesty, shyness

APPENDIX A
LITERAL TRANSLATIONS (APPROXIMATE)
SPANISH-ENGLISH FOR THOSE ENTRIES OF SECTION I
MARKED BY AN ASTERISK (*)
PRECEDING THE ENTRY NUMBER

A

3 You are recommending a good saint (i.e., That's pointless, etc.)

17 Against the hair

51 At the dessert

70 To the four winds

104 By (or with) stone and mud

122 At burned clothing (i.e., Too close to the fire)

181 Eagle or beak (on a coin)

182 Eagle or seal (on a coin)

200 "Chas, Chas" is probably a corruption of the English "Cash, Cash"

210 At the end of the stories

211 From end and head (beginning)

242 At a trot

256 To raise the elbow

257 There at the five-hundreds

B

1 To dance dry

3 Below the ceiling

4 Low neighborhoods

5 Kitchen "battery"

16 Good roots

20 Mouth down

21 Mouth up

C

12 To fall into bed

13 To fall into the story (or account)

15 Coffee only

22 Box of clothes

24 Chicken fever

26 Silence (or hush) the trumpet!

35 To go with feet of lead

43 Face of a heretic

46 To charge (get) with the dead

61 House of the neighborhood

86 To eat at a bad time

91 As God commands

110 Like a visit by the bishop

118 With tongue as a necktie, with tongue on chest

123 With what (kind of) face?

141 Against wind and tide

175 Chinese story

181 To fulfill (complete) years

LL

23 To rain pitchers

M

51 Mid (middle) spoon

56 Memory of (like that of)
a rooster

80 Russian mountain

N

1 To be born standing

7 Knife of (for)
shaving

22 Not to give foot to
the ball (i.e., to
miss kicking the ball)

31 Not to find a ford
(across a stream)

39 It isn't your aunt; your
aunt isn't present

64 Not to be either **chicha**[1]
or lemonade

71 Not to have little hairs
on the tongue

78 Not to have loss or damage

80 Not to have return
of the drop

O

10 Eye of the ox

P

42 To stop dry

45 It seems (to be) a lie

70 Level crossing

72 Feet up

104 Piano with tail

114 To seize or catch
a monkey

116 To paint one a
violin

117 Painter with big
fat brush

125 To iron the seat

144 To place horns on

162 To put feet in "red dust"(?)

Q

24 What fly has bitten you?

45 To be left (to leave one)
squatty or flat

48 To burn the eyelashes

51 With whom are you
interfering (meddling),
Mr. John Big Shot?

R

24 Swirl (whirlpool) of
people

S

66 To be like a fist

76 To be plate of (the)
second table (serving)

79 To be a zero to the left
(of the significant
digits)

80 To be (like) a porcupine

115 Without a shawl (cover)
(i.e., not covered
from view)

---

[1] an alcoholic drink (i.e., "booze")

T

U

V

FOREIGN LANGUAGE REFERENCE BOOKS
FROM PASSPORT BOOKS

Multilingual
The Insult Dictionary:
  How to Give 'Em Hell in 5 Nasty Languages
The Lover's Dictionary:
  How to be Amorous in 5 Delectable Languages

Spanish
Spanish Verbs and Essentials of Grammar
Getting Started in Spanish
Spanish Verb Drills
Guide to Spanish Idioms
Guide to Correspondence in Spanish
Español para los Hispanos

French
Harrap French and English Dictionaries
French Verbs and Essentials of Grammar
Getting Started in French
French Verb Drills

German
New Schöffler-Weis German and English Dictionary
Klett's Super-Mini Dictionary
Getting Started in German
German Verb Drills

Italian
Getting Started in Italian

Russian
Russian Reference Grammar
Business Russian

PASSPORT BOOKS

Trade Imprint of National Textbook Company
Lincolnwood, Illinois U.S.A.